The River

The story of ti
beautiful valley of the
its tributaries from the Vale of Pewsey
to historic Christchurch

by Noreen O'Dell

Photographs by Guy Tanner
and Noreen O'Dell

Cover picture: Breamore Mill

PC

PAUL CAVE
PUBLICATIONS
LTD

Published by Paul Cave Publications Ltd.,
74 Bedford Place, Southampton, SO1 2DF.

Printed by Brown & Son (Ringwood) Ltd., Crowe Arch Lane,
Ringwood, Hants.

NOREEN O'DELL writes of rivers with a warmth and depth of understanding that enables her readers to be absorbed in the atmosphere that she creates.

Her first book — *The River Itchen* — was such a success that BBC TV (South) produced a 30-minute programme showing how Miss O'Dell researched the book during her off-duty spells from being a woman police officer. This delightful television programme created even greater interest in *The River Itchen*.

What an exciting success the *Itchen* proved to be for this exceptionally gifted writer.

Almost equally exciting was the publication of her next book — *The River Test*. This was followed by her delightful *A Hampshire Year* and *Broadlands - Once Upon A Time*. Both were successful, but this did not stop the enthusiastic enquiries — "When is Noreen going to write about another river?"

Of course, it takes a long time to truly research a river, even though Noreen has retired from the police force. I feel sure that you will get great enjoyment from reading *The River Avon*. It is worth waiting for.

Paul Cave

Contents

First Published: November 1991

Introduction

It's a bit of a riddle, the Avon; not a river for those who like a story to have a definite beginning, a clear theme and a neat ending.

Efforts to trace the river north beyond Upavon are met with branching arms to east and west, both marked 'Avon' on the map, yet known by different names locally, and each one dividing again and again. Brian Vesey Fitzgerald, recalling his own rambles in earlier years wrote of chatting to a local sage who told him — 'Thic Avon dussent rise nowhere in a manner of speaking', which put the puzzle in a nutshell.

Even its name adds to the confusion. Flowing for an early part of its life not far from the Bristol Avon, and flirting briefly with the Kennett and Avon Canal, it has for the purpose of identification been called the Hampshire Avon, though much of its greater length is in Wiltshire. Its brooks are numerous, its tributaries long and interesting rivers in themselves.

Beyond Salisbury it loops and divides into numerous channels; and even the end of the Avon is not as tidy as it might be, since it shares the estuary with the Stour at Christchurch — which used to belong to Hampshire, but is now beyond the Dorset boundary!

It's a bit of a riddle, the Avon.

The Source to Upavon

'Moonrakers' they call Wiltshire folk, and long-time inhabitants accept the name with a twinkle in their eye, and just the hint of an artful smile. It's an old tale, and one proving that landlocked counties as well as their coastal neighbours, can have their share of smuggling adventures.

Several streams gather together in the lush Vale of Pewsey, all set to form themselves into the great waterway known as the River Avon, and at the head of the most northerly brook, a soaring spire marks the village of Bishop's Cannings, claimed to be the home of the first Moonrakers.

For smuggled brandy kegs, so goes the story, had been hidden in the village pond, and out on a clear night went the villagers with rakes and hooks to fish them out by the light of the moon. But they were interrupted by a prowling band of Excisemen, who, as Excisemen will, wanted to know the reason for these suspicious nocturnal activities.

The quick-thinking 'yokels', at their most bucolic, waved their rakes at the bright disc reflected in the pond-waters, explaining how they were trying to recover 'thic gurt yaller cheese' which had fallen into the depths. The satisfied Excisemen rode on their way laughing merrily at the foolish ways of rustics, leaving the villagers to celebrate, no doubt, in a manner that seemed satisfactory also to them.

It is fertile country, this Vale of Pewsey, rimmed to the north by rising hills of the Marlborough Downs, with the vast undulating plateau of Salisbury Plain to the south, the whole dotted with interesting and picturesque villages, hamlets, churches and manor houses, and enough thatched rooves to keep those skilful craftsmen in business for life.

Near to Devizes, just south of the A361 that crosses the downs to Swindon, Bishop's Cannings is a straggle of timber frames, red brick and thatch, with nursery-rhyme gardens filled with hollyhocks, asters and larkspur, and a sizeable inn built early this century, its forecourt bright with tubbed marigolds. The handsome grey church of St. Mary is the focal point of the area, a cathedral in miniature, reckoned to be one of the finest in Wiltshire.

Twelfth century fragments form the oldest part of the church, but enlargements, improvements and renovations have continued on and off ever since, and the spire, which at 135 feet is a landmark for miles around, was a 15th century addition that enhanced the overall resemblance to its 'mother church' at Salisbury. St. Mary's is splendid and spacious, cruciform with a lofty arched nave, but imposing and well-preserved though it looks from the outside, death-watch beetle and wet rot are causing havoc within, and an ambitious appeal is in progress.

It is a homely place; a craftsman from Exeter spent many weeks carving each of its many pew-ends with a different design, and earlier, in the 17th century, a pedestal offertory box was hollowed from one solid piece of timber; it bears the marks of three locks required by church laws of the time, a prudent practice whereby keys were held jointly by the vicar and two churchwardens. Earlier still, in a small south chapel, the pale morning light shines on the epitaph of one who died in 1571, quaintly recorded as on 'the firste daie of Februarie.a thousand.five hundred.three score and aleven'.

The infant river is not easy to find, but at the edge of a tussocky field between Bishop's Cannings and the farms of Bourton, a tell-tale ditch is spied, scarcely moist, but tufted with rushes and reeds, dock and sedge, an encouraging clue. By the time it reaches Horton half a mile or so away, the squelchy Avon has grown into a tiny streamlet, a muddy trickle in all but the driest seasons.

Much larger than our Avon here, is the Kennett and Avon Canal which also flows through the village, deep enough to permit the hiring of a rowing boat from the enterprising landlord of the Bridge Inn.

Clear and sparkling along its early route, the little river meanders through meadows and pretty villages: Beechingstoke, with a footpath past the elegant early Georgian manor house, its walls pale-washed, to the charming church with a simple interior, cleanly uncluttered, and on to Marden, from where commences a most pleasant walk through to Wilsford and Charlton and on to Rushall.

Bishop's Cannings Church (G. T.)

Each summer, the tiny rural community of Charlton enjoys a celebration in honour of its 'local lad made good', Stephen Duck, a literary phenomenon of the 18th century.

Born in 1705 to lowly folk, Duck succeeded through his own talent and industry to become court poet, favoured by George II's queen, Caroline of Ansbach. His education was sketchy, his work labouring in the fields, and he committed himself to an early marriage and a young family. But somehow he managed to save what money he could to buy books, painstakingly teaching himself to read with a friend of similar inclinations.

Material was hard to come by, but he was much encouraged by local clergymen, and he was able to collect journals and periodicals, and to study Milton and Dryden. The Reverend Stanley wisely suggested that he should write on subjects he understood, and it was the poem 'The Thresher's Labour' that was to give Duck his popular soubriquet 'the thresher poet'.

Duck's young wife died in 1730, but it was a year of varying fortune; for in the autumn his verses were read to Queen Caroline, a lady of learning and discernment who approved of his work and was impressed by his diligence. She made him a small allowance, gave him a modest house at Richmond and appointed him a Yeoman of the Guard.

Duck became something of a wonder, the talk of London society. Word got around that he was being considered as the next poet laureate. Jealousies abounded, there were petty exchanges and older gentlemen already established in literary circles wrote malicious notes to each other about him — Jonathan Swift, John Gay, and Alexander Pope, although he did change his mind and became something of a friend. The young widower married the Queen's housekeeper at Kew, and was made keeper of the Queen's library at Richmond, but Duck lost his royal patron when Caroline died in 1737.

Nine years afterwards Stephen Duck was ordained and became a preacher at Kew, and later at Byfleet in Surrey. But his tendency to long bouts of depression developed, and in the March of 1756, Stephen Duck of Charlton was found drowned in a river at Reading.

The first Lord Palmerston of Broadlands in Romsey gave a piece of land in his memory, Duck's acre, for the use of local farm labourers, the revenue from which provided funds for an annual 'Duck Feast'. The land has become lost to its original purpose, but the feast survives

White Horse, Milk Hill. (G.T.)

and is a looked-forward-to highlight of Charlton's year — for the men that is, for it is strictly an all-male affair.

Held at the beginning of June at the Charlton Cat Inn, the jollification remembers its famous son in a series of merry traditions; a special barrel of ale is brought in for the occasion, and it is said to be the oldest continuing celebration of its kind in the world.

The Inn used to be the Poore's Arms and its present name is said to have derived from the Charlton Cut, when sheep drovers used the path as a short cut to market. A brick house beside a high bend of the main road from Amesbury to Devizes with long views across the downs, the Inn has a cosy cottage interior, complete with two fluffy black felines, and a spotless dining-room which serves much in the way of home-cooked meals.

Beyond Rushall there is a mingling of streams, for two headwaters are officially recognised for the Avon, the other a dozen or so miles eastwards from Bishop's Cannings across the Vale, past the homesteads of Allington, Stanton St. Bernard, Alton Barnes and Alton Priors, and beyond the little town of Pewsey.

Behind them all sweeps Milk Hill, said to shelter the oldest dewpond in all Britain, and at 964 feet, one of the county's two highest peaks. Into its chalk slope is carved one of the several White Horses of the area, Wiltshire's largest, cut in 1812.

One of the most appealing views of the White Horse is framed by a leaded window of Alton Barnes' tiny Saxon church, set, like its larger sister at Alton Priors a hundred yards away, in the corner of farm fields. These fields are laced with the many trickles from which the village names are derived, ael-tun — village of the waters, and nestling beneath the overhang of a close-growing thicket, bubbles perhaps the clearest, though unofficial, 'head' of the Avon.

From this cool dark pool, still except for the magical ripples rising from springs beneath, starts a cress-filled stream that sets off south under a plank bridge with home-made turnstiles at each end to prevent cattle straying. The bridge interrupts an old and well-maintained cobbled path laid across the meadow at the beginning of the 19th century, for it was a longish walk through tall grass from the rectory to the churches in the fields, and the priest decided that he had conducted enough services with a wet cassock clinging soggily round his ankles.

The road snakes on through Pewsey to the signpost marking Easton Royal, not much more than a single lane ending like others in the valley in footpaths and fields, and edged with the old-fashioned gardens of cottages, Georgian houses and newer bungalows, tall red roses and huge sunflowers nodding against whitewash and brick, tile and thatch.

An old village, Easton, where in 1245 when labourers were poor and itinerants hard put to find sustenance and shelter, a leading landowner founded a hostel, or friary for their aid. Like most such establishments its fortunes ebbed and flowed, but in some manner it thrived until the death of Henry VIII, after which its benefits lapsed.

King Alfred's Statue, Pewsey. (N. O'D.)

The present sturdy church was built in 1591, much altered now and with the unusual Victorian addition of a tower built against the south wall.

It is at Easton Royal that begins the other source of the River Avon. Ponds once claiming to be the main source have long since dried, but all along the lane there remains a dampness here, a trickle there, a puddle or two where sparrows splash and flutter about their ablutions; and then, at the end of the lane, the stream comes into its own where a thoughtfully placed rustic seat made by youngsters from the Youth Opportunities Scheme looks south over the gentle slope of Easton Hill, beech crowned.

The National Grid is much in evidence here and tall pylons and heavy wires tend to mar the beauty, but the gathering swallows find them useful in September, when in the meadows beneath, a few days can change the landscape from a vista of pale standing corn to one of freshly ploughed dark brown furrows, and early walkers who beat the white-woolled sheep to the slopes can be rewarded with a healthy crop of tasty mushrooms.

Westward trickles the stream past the bottom of Milton Lilbourne, whose Friesian herds amble their leisurely way across the main road, keeping to their own pace in lazy disregard of the stockmen who try to chivvy them for the sake of waiting traffic, past Fyfield and Southcott to Pewsey, little 'capital' of the Vale.

A most pleasant country town, Pewsey, with a happy atmosphere, comfortably busy always and downright bustling on Tuesdays when a market is held in the large car park.

At an awkward T-shaped cross-road, a slender statue of King Alfred stands precariously vulnerable to traffic. To anyone familiar with the massive granite and bronze tribute to the warrior-monarch at Winchester, Pewsey's seems modest indeed, with the king a slight crowned figure, simply clad, but if it is unassuming in stature, its various inscriptions are stirring stuff, reminding folk that the king was a chief landowner in the Vale, and 'fought nobly for his country's benefit'. It was erected in the summer of 1913 to commemorate the coronation two years earlier of King George V 'who grandly follows in great King Alfred's footsteps'.

12

The Avon at Pewsey. (N. O'D.)

The Avon flows through Pewsey, draped with a graceful willow in front of picture-book cottages, and southwards towards Upavon, already large enough to provide a desirable residence for a family of moorhens.

Much of the land hereabouts belongs to Rushall Farm, 1,650 chemical-free acres supporting livestock, arable fields and cereals, probably the largest organic farm in our islands; not a new venture, the land has been without synthetic additives for twenty years.

The farm has its own stone-mill where the wholesome harvest is ground with all its goodness intact, and callers are welcome to visit and buy the whole-wheat flour, which twice a week is made into loaves and scones at the mill bake-house. Some of the fields grow barley, and an imported pearling machine discards the husks and turns the grain into pearl barley which is also on sale to callers, in quantities large and small.

The two streams from east and west converge on this natural farmland just before Scales Bridge at Upavon, uniting to form the one River Avon, sweeping grandly towards the coast.

Upavon to Amesbury

A larger village, Upavon, than others in the Vale, with a quite different pace, the main A345 running through. A gentle village though, with small shops and cottages of all sorts, some with bulging timber-framed walls, some with straw birds topping thatched ridges, and newer housing behind them.

The brick Antelope Hotel with its elegant Georgian frontage faces the pale-washed Ship Inn, sailing-ship sign swinging, and above the rooftops, the river beyond, rises the 13th century tower of Upavon's strong parish church.

Eastward across the river, the R.A.F. are established on the windswept crown of that delightful contradiction, Upavon Down. With brick buildings on one side of the road and draughty hangars on the other, R.A.F. Upavon is the oldest station still in use, the Royal Flying Corps having had a school for pilots there in 1912. 'The Father of the Royal Air Force' was the station's first Assistant Commandant, then Major Trenchard, later to become Chief of Air Staff. The first night landing to be made in England was at Upavon in 1913, and it was at one time responsible for training all R.A.F. flying instructors.

Upavon has housed many famous units over the years, and is now home to Headquarters No.1 Group Strike Command, with the major responsibilities of providing Attack Forces, Air-to-Air refuelling and other support and transport roles including the Queen's Flight.

If there is an Upavon, then downstream, past pretty riverside villages, there must be a Netheravon. Take a wrong turning there and the way is firmly barred by the white-painted gates of another airfield, guarded by blue-bereted soldiers of the Army Air Corps. Lynx and Gazelle helicopters buzz over the camp, in which are the Support Weapons Wing and a training ground for the School of Infantry.

Back on the right track again, the lane leads to a bridge overlooking a tall brick building known as The Old Mill. There was indeed a corn-mill there once, water-driven, with its great wheels turning until the early years of this century. By then like so much of Salisbury

Plain, it had been acquired by the War Department, and its purpose changed in 1914 when the present building was put up as an electricity generating station, with a water-turbine and diesel engines, later displaced by electricity from the National Grid.

Its uses between the wars were varied, mostly providing entertainment for the community, dances, boxing matches, and a cinema showing flickering silent films. Light industry followed, and in 1984 'Wiltshire's youngest brewery' was born there, the small private Bunce's Brewery, producing draught beer by the tried and true methods of tradition: Bunce's Best Bitter, distributed to Free Houses over a fifty-mile radius from Bath to Guildford.

The tall building facing the road, with its ready-installed haulage equipment made ideal premises, and the top floor was converted into open-plan living accommodation for the husband and wife entrepreneurs, Tony and Robin Bunce. Now within are the mellow brewing scents of fermenting English hops and high-quality malt, and without, a sedate family of swans glide gracefully in the mill-pond; the grey-green eggs were hatched in nearby reeds months earlier, a miracle witnessed through binoculars from the mill's top floor.

The river is deep here, and smooth, shiny as agate, dark, polished as obsidian; it is not a working river, for it is has no use in the brewery, merely providing a backcloth of peace and long pastoral views east and northward to the grey church among the trees.

Broad now, the Avon flows on through Figheldean with colourful gardens, hanging baskets and pavement tubs. Across the leaf-spattered lane from the church, cottages are shaded by a giant spreading chestnut tree, whereunder, an octogenarian exile remembers, stood the forge of the village blacksmith, a scene straight from Longfellow's pen. His father was apprenticed to the 'smith in his early days, and he well remembers pumping the bellows to rouse the glowing coals, a pleasing cameo of village history.

Joseph Addison knew this part of the Avon in a different age, for he was born at Milston in 1672, when his father was rector of the charming flint and stone church there. Addison was to use his abilities well, becoming a notable Whig politician and contributing to the world of journalism, theatre, poetry and essays; Jonathan Swift, Richard Steele, William Congreve and he were young men together.

Perhaps his rural upbringing influenced his outlook on life, for Addison was to write later of his own home, 'I value my garden more for being full of blackbirds than of cherries, and very frankly give them fruit for their song.'

At Durrington the river has seen many years of change. An ancient bank and ditch, Durrington Walls, enclose thirty acres of history, wherein were once various circular structures with post-holes for timbers, not dissimilar to the site of Woodhenge just across the busy A345; that monument is perhaps a little disappointing, though no doubt of much interest to the knowledgeable, unique and probably older than the magical Stonehenge a few miles to the west, but with none of the charismatic draw of that vast, emotive and very visible mystery.

Remnants of a medieval Durrington with its sizeable village cross bring life nearer to the present day, as do the ritual Maypole celebrations which took place on May 13th, the old May Day, until only a few generations ago.

Now much of the old village has been gobbled up by the modern army community, for in a loop of the Avon is Bulford, one of the biggest garrisons in Wiltshire, Headquarters of the Army South West District.

The old village was quiet once, with its Norman-towered church, gabled and mullioned manor-house, and its pretty riverside walk joined by the little 'Nine Mile River', sometimes called the Avon's only true tributary. Now it has been swamped by the mile-square camp beneath Beacon Hill, with brick buildings and rows of huts sprawling among the maze of roads carrying green service vehicles, and the large no-nonsense garrison church of St. George, built in 1927.

The 2nd Battalion of the Royal Regiment of Fusiliers live here, proud red hackles in their berets, the Allied Mobile Force for rapid deployment in times of tension. A part of NATO's flanks, they act in a deterrent role, training in snow vehicles during Norway's arctic winter, and in summer tackling the burning heat of Turkey.

Into the steep side of Beacon Hill while they were stationed at Bulford, New Zealand troops of the First World War cut the 'Bulford

Kiwi', still a landmark at 420 feet long, its bill alone 150 feet, the letters 'N.Z' beneath; a change from White Horses.

Away to the west of the Avon stretches Salisbury Plain with its major involvement in the armed services, its long straight roads undulating across wide open views of flocks and crops, and the odd cluster of military buildings. Tanks lumber across distinctive yellow-marked tracks, with warnings of greasy roads in wet weather, red danger flags dot the edge of the firing ranges, and the putter of small arms practice with the occasional heavier thud accompanies passing traffic.

For Larkhill houses the Royal School of Artillery, teaching the use of rifles, light machine guns and small arms. There are ranges throughout the Avon Valley — the 'Range Road' they call it, through from Bulford to Tidworth.

Off-duty soldiers wanting a change from the army environment head for Amesbury, the first town of any size in the upper Avon Valley, busy capital of the Plain.

So manifold are the age-old relics on the chalk Plain, the barrows, earthworks and ancient trackways, that the date of Amesbury is difficult to pinpoint, but there are indications of a settled population well before 2,000 BC, possibly one or even two thousand years before, making it one of our earliest townships. Easy fording of the river and a crossing of tracks from north to south and east to west have ensured its continued growth and prosperity, especially after the establishment of a direct route from London to Exeter.

On a terrace west of the river a busy Iron Age hill fort throve, known now as Vespasian's Camp, although it was whimsically misnamed and has no known association with that 1st-century emperor.

The modern name, which over the years has been recorded as various versions of Ambrosbury, is said to have been derived from Ambrosius Aurelianus, a soldier in Roman Britain of the 5th century, said to have been born and buried there; some have claimed that he was an 'uncle' of King Arthur.

Saxon victors of a battle at Old Sarum in 552, who, according to the Anglo-Saxon Chronicles 'defeated the indigenous population', stayed on in the area and may well have moved up-river to settle at Amesbury.

In those far-off days a Priory had been built, and in the many legends of Arthur, his widow Guinevere retired there when he died. When in time her life too was ended, the devoted Lancelot had her body removed for safety and 'led her sombre funeral procession over the downs to Glastonbury'.

In 979 another abbey was founded and occupied until Henry VIII's 'dissolution' when it was destroyed, and the estates granted to the land-hungry Duke of Somerset.

The little community of Amesbury flourished through the Middle Ages. One of its most important industries after the introduction of tobacco in 1570 was the making of clay pipes, local quarries providing a clay of particularly high quality. The pipes were popular until about sixty years ago, but the business heyday was the 17th century. Tributes were generous, 'best for shape and colour' and 'the best tobacco pipes in England'; in 1651 the Duke of Bedford had a regular order by the gross, at 18/6d a time.

The 3rd Duke of Queensberry inherited the estate in 1725 with his wife 'Kitty', a hearty hostess of London society's literary favourites which included John Gay, who is said to have taken himself off to an ornamental cavern in the grounds to write perhaps his best known work 'The Beggar's Opera'.

The Duke instigated various projects at Amesbury, and built the mellow stone five-arched Queensberry Bridge, the Avon winding beneath.

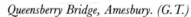

Queensberry Bridge, Amesbury. (G.T.)

Amesbury to Salisbury

The valley between Amesbury and Salisbury must be some of the most beautiful countryside in all England, the serene Woodford Valley, everyone's romantic dream of rich pastoral perfection. The river is wide and deep, curving lazily through lush green fields and thickly wooded banks.

Any sheltered bend is like a busy nursery in mid-summer. Coots, white-pated, patrol their territory, each with half-dozen or so young, growing now, but looking strangely incomplete with their lack of tails, a pale, downy charcoal-grey, with smooth heads showing no trace of their knobbly pink kindergarten top-knots. A moorhen strides along the undergrowth topping the bank, its splayed yellow feet moving firmly on the slippery slope, a sooty chick nearly as big as itself hurrying alongside, still demanding to be fed.

A family of ducks hug the bank, almost invisible in their camouflage, the babes brown, fore-shortened versions of their parents, dipping and upending, while with a plop a little grebe disappears beneath the olivine surface, to re-appear yards away when expectation of seeing it again has almost gone.

Great drifts of shaggy weed make islands in the current, sometimes centred with an untidy splodge of a nest, built with infinite patience a month before while mum sat upon her eggs, and dad brought an endless supply of twigs and reeds, passing them from beak to beak and away again, too busy foraging to watch as the new season's housewife tucked and tweaked and wove them into place. The titivating and patching-up still goes on, as the second brood open and shut their baby beaks, emitting squeals and mews like a basket full of kittens.

Nearby, on his own gently-spinning green 'island', a handsome mallard drake balances one-legged as he preens, blues and greens dazzling, soft feathers catching in the pale haze of water forget-me-nots as they float ashore.

Huge limes and willows drape the far bank, alive with magpies and clattering pigeons, while nearer, chaffinches scavenge among the hawthorn, coal-tits hang upside down in the nut-trees, and a perky wren nearly bursts his heart with a song out of all proportion to his tiny size.

The wide riverside is a profusion of alder and hazel and rowan; dog-roses and honeysuckle trail among the huge branching umbels of hogweed seven feet high, tangling with lacy cow-parsley, wild angelica, comfrey and figwort; nearer the ground, bees drone in the clover and in the quiet of noon can be heard the clicking and chinking of innumerable insects going about their lives unseen.

Suddenly, heart stoppingly, the sky is ripped in two as a sleek jet zips overhead with a thunderous, screaming roar, for the test base of Boscombe Down is only a hike away. The idyll which had seemed so eternal is splintered into fragments, a sharp bringing-up-to-date in this tranquil interlude of yesteryear.

The whole valley is rich in manors and country houses, some grand, some modest, Wilsford, Lake and Heale House among the best known.

Wilsford Manor was built early this century, using carefully retained grey Tisbury stone and knapped flint from the old farmhouse it replaced. The architect was Detmar Blow, whose influence is found everywhere in the valley, commissioned at Wilsford by Sir Edward and Lady Tennant to create a mellow manor house in the Jacobean style. Sir Edward's fortune came from his great-grandfather's factory just outside Glasgow, which made use of the newly invented powdered bleach, patented in 1799. Lady Tennant had been Pamela Wyndham, whose portrait with her two sisters by John Stringer Sargent was to become known as 'The Three Graces'.

Stephen Tennant was the youngest of their five children, one of the 'Bright Young People' of the '20's; 'dear, strange, beautiful, gifted Stephen', his close friend Vita Sackville-West was to call him; 'one of the more bizarre figures' commented a London newspaper. Artist,

Opposite: Woodford Valley.

20

painter, poet and diarist, he was of a circle which included Rex Whistler, Siegfried Sassoon, Cecil Beaton and William Walton.

Wilsford was elaborately furnished, the decor sometimes styled by Syrie Maugham, often from Tennant's own sketches and designs. Less frivolous were the dark years of the last war, when the Red Cross ran a hospital there.

Regaining possession, Tennant threw off all the gloomy associations and entered wholeheartedly into the redecoration of his beloved home and the re-stocking of his garden, using all his unbridled artistic flair and extraordinary talents, his ideas exotic and striking, sometimes chic, often outlandish and outrageous.

Stephen Tennant died, a self-styled 'legend', early in 1987, just into his sixties, and at the auction of Wilsford and its contents, the world had an opportunity to witness a lifestyle few could match.

Lovely Lake House overlooking the river, has its origins in the 16th century, but like others in the valley has been much altered and restored by the skilful craftsmanship of Detmar Blow. Sadly, much of the work was in vain and the house was gutted by fire in 1912, but was rebuilt in attractive grey chequering in flint and stone, a pattern familiar in this area, with tall chimneys and high gables.

Heale House, approached by a long dappled avenue of tall poplars, looks much the same as when it was built about 1640, despite a disastrous fire last century, and has an exciting tale to tell of the troubled Stuart times.

The Civil War was long over, and Charles I had been executed two years before, in 1649; Cromwell had routed the Royalists at the Battle of Worcester, and Charles II was fleeing to the safety of France, for his life was in great danger; few knew his whereabouts.

Heale was in the possession of the Hyde family, kinsmen of Edward Hyde, a trusted adviser of the king, later the 1st Earl of Clarendon, and in 1651, Mrs. Amphillis Hyde, a widow, was living there.

When two riders came up to her door at dusk, she recognised one as the royal fugitive. She was very ready to provide him with sanctuary, but it was not a simple matter, for Roundhead troops were garrisoned at Salisbury, and the Heale servants could not be depended upon for loyalty to the Crown.

The king and his companion were accommodated overnight, but advised to set out next morning as if continuing on their journey and to return in secrecy at night. And so the king rode out to take a tourist's look at Stonehenge, and when the servants had taken themselves off for an evening of jollity at Salisbury fair, he returned and remained 'in the hiding hole that was very convenient and safe, and staid there all alone some four or five days . . .', attended by Mrs Hyde and her discreet sister.

Thirty years later in more settled days, Charles recounted the tale to friends who included Samuel Pepys, and the diarist jotted down the king's words in his own form of shorthand, the original document being kept in the Pepys' library at Cambridge.

When in due course horses were brought to the gate for the king's next move, one of the pack-animals broke loose and was lost in the water-meadows before being recaptured. Recently, a horse-shoe was fished out of the river there, and after investigation by the British Museum, is thought to have been thrown by the wayward pack-horse in his moments of freedom.

There followed several changes of family and the fire which destroyed much of the house, and in 1894 it was bought by the Hon. Louis Greville, great-uncle of the present owner; with the co-operation once again of the busy Detmar Blow, he set about the sensitive rebuilding of Heale House to its original pattern, using contemporary materials and designs inside and out, and restoring the eight acres of gardens.

Early in the century, Louis Greville spent some time in Tokyo on diplomatic service, and brought home with him several grand mementoes, two of which feature in the garden — an unusual eight tatami Japanese tea-house with rice-paper shutters, and a small version of the Nikko Bridge, bringing a touch of 'Willow Pattern' to this quintessentially English valley.

Japanese Tea House and Bridge, Heale House Garden. (N.O'D.)

Now Major David and Lady Anne Rasch live at Heale, and have opened their delightful garden to the public. Carrier streams from the main river meander through the lawns, and informal arrangements on different levels are a joy of clematis and honeysuckle, pinks, hostas, delphiniums and the most wonderful roses; there are old round box bushes, avenues of apple trees, a mulberry, walnut, medlar and spindle, magnolias and cherries; so much.

In 1984, Christies and the Historic Houses Association got together to organise an award for the Garden of the Year, and the first winner of their much sought-after plaque, was this altogether charming and imaginative garden at Heale.

These lovely old houses look across the Avon to a string of hamlets and villages on the east bank. Great Durnford is tucked neatly into a snug valley, the river beside it '. . . abounding in troutes catched by speare in the night . . .', when diarist John Evelyn was there in the 17th century.

Lord Tryon and his family have their country home at Durnford, in nearby Ogbury House, the manor having been purchased in 1870, and the church walls shelter memorials to the first and second barons.

St. Andrew's is well concealed, its grey tower clearly visible from the high approach road into the valley, but less easy to find in the village itself.

Above the aged wooden door, lovingly handled by many generations, is an unusual tympanum of diamond chequering in green and white stone, a combination favoured by Norman craftsmen in this area, green sandstone from Hurdcott and white Chilmark stone, under the arch of a carved frieze.

Inside, as might be expected in so old a church there is much of interest, including large remains of wall-paintings from perhaps the 13th century; but one treasure visitors and villagers can no longer enjoy, for a notice on the lectern reports with sorrow, the theft of a priceless Chained Book of 1571, which had lain there for four hundred years until the sad day in 1970 when a visitor abused the hospitality of Durnford's secluded church.

While some villages have grown over the years, others have diminished in size.

In the 1920s, when Edith Olivier, a Woodford lady from Daie House, gathered together local tales which she called 'Moonrakings' from older folk in the valley, tiny Netton was remembered as a larger community, through whose lanes passed drovers and their flocks from distant farms. 'One enterprising lady,' wrote Miss Olivier, '. . . would have ready outside her house a small table with cakes and bread and cheese, and by the side a cask of ale, so that the drovers could stop and partake of light refreshments, also to exchange news . . .'

A welcome interlude for hot and thirsty shepherds, and rewarding for the old lady to see her provisions gratefully snapped up while she listened to the comfortable chatter of daily doings other than her own. Enterprising indeed, for it is a quiet valley, with only the homesteads of Salterton and Little Durnford along the four-mile stretch to the great cathedral city.

The River Bourne

The Avon is well-supplied with water from smaller rivers to the west, but the eastern side has only one major tributary, and that not very useful since much of its length is dry until the rains of winter.

It starts, the Bourne, from a rushy pond at Burbage, a village south of the Savernake Forest and once part of it; Hungerford ten miles, Marlborough six, says the signpost at the crossroads, and only a mile from Easton Royal; a choice of inns lie along its main street, the White Hart, Three Horseshoes, and less traditionally named Bullfinch.

The ditch follows a field course to Collingbourne Kingston, a few homes gathered round the church, twenty names on the little cenotaph shaded by old trees at the gate, some from the same family; twenty of its best men, a devastating loss for a small rural community.

An impressive and colourful monument in the church reaches from floor to ceiling and remembers the Pile family, Sir Thomas and his wife Elizabeth and their son, Sir Gabriel and wife, Dame Anne, with two kneeling figures said to represent sons, erected in 1646. The Pile family were substantial landowners and had a house near the church which gave a right of presentation to the living, and to take tithes.

A pretty stretch is Sunton, a charming backwater, not much more than an informal row of cottages and houses of brick and flint, colour-

Sunton. (N. O'D.)

wash and thatch, with fat ducks squatting on front lawns on one side of a narrow no-through lane just wide enough for a vehicle, and the Bourne ditch on the other; a private place, crouching secretively behind the main road.

Collingbourne Ducis, once part of the Duchy of Lancaster is spread around the junction of two main roads, and the church, in a quiet corner, has the unsual novelty of having a tower whose upper slopes double as a dovecote, with purpose-built nest-holes.

And then it's back to the army again at Tidworth, the other end of the 'Range Road' from Larkhill, across Beacon Hill from Bulford, North Tidworth in Wiltshire and South Tidworth in Hampshire.

Like Bulford, Tidworth is a garrison town, with its own church among the trees and a well-tended cemetery overlooking peaceful downs; as well as the barracks there are married quarters, a shopping centre, health clinic, entertainments and sports fields. The garrison is part of the United Kingdom Mobile Forces housing the 1st Infantry Brigade, and provides a NATO reinforcement role in the Baltic approaches, with logistical back up.

Despite the busy-ness, it is all surprisingly peaceful, the Bourne sparkling across the green backed by tree-clad hills, their autumn colours glowing in mellow October sunlight, with sounds faintly borne on the wind of band practice and bugle calls, and less attractive, the putter of gunfire.

At Shipton Bellinger the stream moves sluggishly beneath the lane, and after a short sojourn in Hampshire returns to Wiltshire beside the main road at Cholderton, a ditch often dry, choked with dock and nettles, valerian and convolvulus. On one side of the small roundabout a handsome clock tops a brick house, and opposite, the 18th-century Crown, whitewashed and thatched, with dark-painted shutters, welcomes travellers.

Cholderton's rather stark grey church, a small bell-turret at the corner, stands high at the end of a short gravel lane, with low cottages on one side, tiny windows peeping from under the thatch, and a sturdy flint school-house, now a private home on the other.

A large lychgate and yew-lined path leads to the heavy west door, whose sturdily-wrought key is a weighty affair, twelve inches long and thick as a finger.

The church replaced a Saxon building, pulled down to make way for the vision of Thomas Mozley, its energetic new rector. Mrs. Mozley, whose brother was John Henry Newman, later to become Cardinal Newman, laid the foundation stone in 1841, and the rector supervised all stages of the planning and building of the church. He nearly bankrupted himself by providing £5,000 of the £6,000 cost of the project; the roof, together with a band of carpenters to install it, he had brought by land and water from Ipswich, where he found it mouldering on the quay, and he interested himself in the window designs, searching and sketching what he saw on his travels.

Work was held up for two months when a homeless local poacher camped in the spacious porch with his young family, fastening a piece of sail-cloth across the entrance to keep out the winter wind.

Yet for all the rector's zeal and enthusiasm, the church has a chill air, the only warmth coming from the bright windows in which he delighted.

A later rector had his own sadness, a wall-tablet remembering John King, his only son, 2nd Lieutenant in the R.F.C., killed aged nineteen in October 1918, so very near the end of hostilities and coming of the peace for which he fought.

Any land of Wiltshire's antiquity must have its share of mysteries and legends, and ghost stories abound among older residents in this wooded area.

Ralph Whitlock in his 'Folklore of Wiltshire', tells of the curate who walks the village of Allington; it had been officially recorded that the young man fell when mounting his horse after visiting friends and broke his neck, but later, when on her deathbed a woman indicated her wish to tell the true story, she took a sudden turn for the worse and died before she could do so.

Mr. Whitlock tells also of the poltergeist which took possession of a cottage bread oven at Newton Tony, but the village has another more earthly claim to fame, for that tireless 17th-century traveller, Celia Fiennes was born there; the church has a memorial to her, and descendants of her family still go adventuring today.

Boscombe's old rectory too, is said to have its ghost, but the flint and stone church is quaintness itself. St. Andrew's has a simple 14th-century nave and chancel, a time when texts were illustrated on the walls, and a small part of the Fourth Commandment shows through later re-decoration.

The eminent theologian, Richard Hooker, was rector at Boscombe at the end of the 16th century, and it is said that so many countrymen flocked from miles around to hear his sermons, that a north transept was built to accommodate them, but in fact the date of the addition is very likely to be a little after his incumbency. Isaac Walton was also rector there for a year in 1679, son of the 'compleat angler', Izaak Walton.

In high-backed box pews of the 17th century, family seats are arranged in a square, where members sit in total seclusion, overlooked only by the preacher from his three-decker pulpit bearing the date 1633, gained by a rather hazardous stairway, a tester above; below, a heavy bible, brass-edged, lies on the lectern.

Just beyond the little wooden bell-tower runs a dry ditch where when the rains come, will flow the Bourne. The village lies just off the main road, in a corner unexpectedly quiet, until abruptly, unseen, the deep echoing roar of throbbing engines vibrates on the air, a crescendo that shatters the peace. And once again Boscombe Down, just beyond the trees, is the culprit.

Old and new sit often together in Wiltshire, and Boscombe Down is responsible for a good deal of the noise in its skies; the Aeroplane and Armament Experimental Establishment have their base there, their business being to test aircraft, components and equipment before acceptance by the R.A.F. The fliers are R.A.F. men, graduates of Boscombe's own Empire Test Pilot School, and they rely on civilian ground and support staff of the Ministry of Defence.

Boscombe's planes can be recognised by their red, white and blue livery, and conspicuous too, are the lumbering old yellow Harvards, low-flying, used mostly for the photographing of aircraft trials.

Lynx helicopters and Sea Kings add to the racket, and the distinctive deep chatter of the double-rotor Chinooks, but noisiest of all, and it has to be said, most fascinating, are the Tornedos and Harriers that tear open the skies as they flash across the heavens, twisting and turning with grace and speed and elegance, a free display of the skill and devilment of their pilots.

Porton is another of the Wiltshire villages whose name is now better known for its Defence associations, and has changed because of it.

The straight downland road to the east is fenced, a long driveway at right-angles flanked by tall wide gates bearing an arbitrary warning that the road may be closed without notice, a stark reminder that this is Ministry land.

For on Porton Down, to combat the German use of gas against our troops at Ypres, 3,000 acres were acquired for the purpose of investigating defensive and offensive methods.

From that small beginning in 1916 has grown the Chemical Defence Establishment, the United Kingdom's research centre for 'Studying the Threat and Developing the Defence'; offensive work was abandoned in 1957.

Now, gases in warfare are only a part of Porton's programme, as scientists study the environmental hazards of pollution and toxic chemicals, and the problems arising from them — decontamination, treatment of casualties and the development of protective gear on behalf of the emergency services and industry; world health problems are also investigated, and the various units work on detection, analysis, assessment and trials, enormously diverse work involving scientific, engineering and technical skills.

The ranges have more than doubled their acreage in the intervening years, and with so much downland and scrub inaccessible to the encroachment of progress, the land around the Establishment has become a major conservation area, carefully monitored by its own enthusiastic groups, with two public nature trails through Isle of Wight Woods and over Roche Court Down.

Much of the tussocky grassland has lain undisturbed for a couple of centuries, and some has probably never seen a plough, making it a rare site of archaeological interest and for natural life, cropped regularly by rabbits, a haven for badgers and occasionally roe deer.

All ages of our old civilization are represented in the relics of Porton, the oldest find a flint hand-axe used perhaps an incredible 100,000 years ago, when man and beast could trek across the European continent from the south coast to the north, and long before the melting Ice Ages made an island of our country.

Remains of two separate flint-mines, each with more than a hundred 'shafts', little more than depressions now, are reckoned to be the most important Neolithic industrial site known in Britain, worked about 2,500 BC. It also boasts the second largest bell barrow in Wiltshire with a height of nearly 18ft and a diameter of more than 102ft, and round barrows are dotted all over the area, with signs of the settlements of Bronze Age people, Iron Age earthworks, Roman pottery and Saxon burials.

Over all this age-old history fly the birds of Porton, many familiar to any rambler, several less so, the more encouraging because of breeding successes; ground-nesting birds are especially at home on this very private land, like the wheatear, and more rare still, the elusive stone-curlew, whose growing population is a joy to watchers, but others are equally content, whinchats, warblers, pipits and yellowhammers; owls, hawks and buzzards.

A population which might be thought to have grown enough is the yellow ant, a density unmatched in the country. The 'ant-scape' of Roche Court Down holds three million mounds as big as mole-hills, housing an estimated thirty-five billion ants, a never-ending supply to delight the resident green woodpeckers.

Fungi thrive too, common and uncommon, there for the finding; rounded penny-buns, field mushrooms, dainty fairy-rings, slate-coloured wood blewitt, puff-balls, lawyer's wigs, fluted cups of lactaria, and red-brown slabs of beefsteak. Edible those, but better left alone are the bright false chanterelles, stinkhorn, and sickener, pale stalks topped with scarlet cap, and prettiest — and deadliest — of all, white-spotted red fly-agaric, panther-cap, destroying-angel, and death cap.

Porton has a vast plantation of spiky juniper, evergreen, with dark pungent berries, and dogwood, red-branching, sweet-briar, elder, yew; and buckthorn, its small black berries sharply purgative.

Wild flowers too, some rarely seen, bloom freely on these downs; orchids of all sorts, fairy flax, carline and musk thistle, tway-blade, squinancy wort; and meadow clary, rarest of all, with deep violet flower spikes, much protected, the water-soaked seed once sought after for treatment of sore eyes. Other names are more familiar — cranesbill, columbine, thyme, marjoram, mullein, mignonette, cowslip, harebell and hound's-tongue, a catalogue of delightful old names.

31

And where flowers grow in undisturbed profusion, so will come the butterflies, several fritillaries, orange-brown with dark spots, so alike that only the dedicated can tell the difference; skippers, large and small, the common meadow browns, ringlets and speckled woods, coppers, hair-streaks and commas; and even a colony of the grandly named Duke of Burgundy, though but a poor relation of more spectacular tropical butterflies.

There is more to Porton than the bleak brick and huts of the Establishment and a lot to be said for keeping even the most well-meaning of humans at bay.

By now the Bourne is flowing well, a full-grown brook shimmering through the three little Winterbourne communities of Winterbourne Gunner, Winterbourne Dauntsey, and Winterbourne Earls, all in a row.

The bridge carrying the A30 road from London across the Bourne bears the name of Thomas à Becket, St. Thomas's Bridge, for he was a 'curé-priest' at Winterbourne, probably at St. Mary's; during this time the saint was engaged in a deep quarrel with Henry II when he visited the great palace of Clarendon in the forest away to the east, over constitutional differences between church and state.

There are only three more names now before the city, Ford, through which Roman travellers splashed on their way from Winchester to Old Sarum, Milford and Laverstock, two villages grown larger with new developments.

In the green triangle before the Bourne joins with the Avon, ancient and modern were once again only a stone's throw apart. For nearby hangars tell of a war-time airfield, where planes circled above the fifty-six acres of their neighbouring earthwork as its builders could never have done, and look down on the Iron Age hill fort which is Old Sarum.

A peaceful place, Sarum, where the lucky walker can stand and listen to the silence, a rare experience; sometimes there is a hum of traffic from the road to Salisbury, and of course, Boscombe Down is only a few seconds away as the jet flies; but sometimes, just sometimes, there is a blessed silence.

Old Sarum is one of those places whose beginnings are shrouded in the mists of pre-history, but certainly on the old site a simple defensive hill-fort was built by men of the Iron Age. Romans looked

Old Sarum (Eric Hills).

it over, approved the strategic advantage of the intercrossing tracks large and small, called it Sorviodunum and made themselves a community of modest importance, probably just to the south of the hill, nearer to Stratford sub-Castle.

The name changed according to the residents, Saxons, Danes and Normans. There may have been a church there early in the 8th century; King Alfred thought it was a place worth fortifying and King Edgar travelled there to hold a Parliament in 960, by which time it was becoming an established township.

And then came William; he liked Sarum. He chose the breezy hill site to muster his conquering troops in 1070 at the end of the long campaign of subjection. The episcopal see was transferred from Sherborne, and a new cathedral was started with Osmund, a relative of William, as bishop.

Osmund also built a castle, of earth and timber, strengthened with stone a hundred or so years later. It was the conflict between the inhabitants of these two major buildings, combined with difficulties with the water supply, which brought about the end of Old Sarum.

The clerics of the bishop's cathedral were at loggerheads with the soldiers of the castle, who harassed them at every opportunity, and eventually the clergy took themselves off two miles down the valley to start a new cathedral where all rivers meet, at New Sarum. At a distance of nearly eight hundred years such squabbling within one small community seems so very silly, but 'twas ever thus.

Now both the cathedral and the castle are long since gone, and the town and the people; but the age-old ramparts and ditches have survived, with yard-thick lines of the flint castle wall, and the outline of the cathedral clearly marked, all open upon payment to visitors.

The City of New Sarum, Salisbury, went from strength to strength, and is open to visitors too!

Photograph: Peter Charman.

The River Wylye (and Till)

Upwards through the little string of Deverills, from near to the Somerset border flows the new River Wylye, a fisherman's river, its course taking it through a lovely valley backed by steep chalk escarpments, some grass-covered, some with vast armies of ancient trees camped on their slopes. The longest of the Avon's tributaries and with one of its own, it also carries the greatest volume of clear sparkling water. No Winterbourne, the Wylye.

Known to some here as the Deverill, the cressy stream huddles close to the four villages of Kingston Deverill, Monkton Deverill, Brixton Deverill and Longbridge Deverill, in whose church lies Sir John Thynne, builder of the great mansion of Longleat. How surprised he would have been to know that three hundred years on there would be lions, giraffes and ostriches roaming his land, and muddy hippopotami wallowing in his waters. Perhaps though, since Sir John has been 'seen' at Longleat on various occasions over the centuries, he does know, and watches with the visitors.

The little Wylye by-passes Warminster away to the north-west and turns east towards Boreham and Bishopstrow, where Aldhelm, whose missions in the 7th century did so much for churches in the West Country, stayed to preach. During his sermon he stuck his staff in the ground, whereupon, legend has it, the gathering was amazed to witness its wondrous growth into a thriving ash tree. A miracle indeed, and the church there is dedicated to the saint.

Norton Bavant is next, approved by William Cobbett on his travels as 'one of the prettiest spots that my eyes ever beheld', and on to Heytesbury, a rather grey little town high at the edge of the Plain, the busy A36 running through; an octagonal lock-up is built into the high wall at the roadside, of much the same date as nearby almshouses, rebuilt after a fire in 1770. There are many interesting tales of history in the buildings of Heytesbury and an impressive church above the river.

A number of small villages edge both sides of the Wylye. Knook, a Celtic name, three single-splayed windows in its tiny Norman church, and the treasure of an intricately carved tympanum, a little the worse for age and weather, over the blocked-up south door. Room for fifty or so here, called to worship by a single bell, its rope dangling in the porch. It has a friendly atmosphere, with Easter flowers arranged in a stout jug placed conveniently in the font.

And Upton Lovell, named after the Lovel family, long-time owners of local land, a Lovel House still fronting the lane and monuments in the church. A family feeling here too, outside, the lawns starred with primroses and blue anemones, while within, the wide stone windowsills and wooden font-cover are decorated with imaginative Easter gardens of moss and spring blossoms, pretend chicks and real eggs. No baptisms at Upton Lovell during Eastertide! Even the cold effigy of a long-dead knight is cheered by a bright posy placed on his armorial breastplate, a thoughtful gesture.

The font itself is a precious Saxon bowl, discovered among the dusty jumble of a barn, and re-erected on a later stem.

A narrow meandering lane, a railway crossing and a bridge lead south of the river, skirted by villages trailing one from another, tiny Corton, and Boyton between high banks, plump ginger-haired sows browsing behind the hedge; the swell of a green ridge at Sherrington, and Stockton, rather larger, a gabled late-Elizabethan manor set back from the lane, old almshouses and cottages, an ancient church and a wealth of seasonal traditions and customs enjoyed over its long past.

The river loops north to the main road, where traffic spoils Codford St. Peter and St. Mary, although a charming Saxon panel in the sanctuary of the roadside St. Peter's, believed to be part of a 9th century cross, is well worth a pause.

Fisherton looks down on the river, with Bapton and Deptford to follow on opposite sides, and a turning off an awkward junction leads to Wylye, a pleasant leafy village with the river at its edge, and not a yellow line in sight.

The churning water gushes under an old grist mill now in private hands, guarded by a sea-sprite. A statue anyway, full-sized, collected in Italy on a Grand Tour to grace Wilton House in the 18th century, and given by a grateful Earl of Pembroke to honour the memory of a coachman, who drowned at the spot while saving the life of one his family. The treasure has more than once been in danger of being swept away, and a small island has been built to divert the fierce rush of water around it.

In St. Mary's just off the main street, half a dozen or so bell-ringers practice beneath the square tower, tugging and looping their ropes and sallies while the bells swing above them, and a black cat strolls in through the porch door to listen; and those who thirst after righteousness can take themselves round the corner to the Bell Inn, a hostelry familiar to the coaching trade of three centuries.

At the other end of the Domesday village, a United Reform Church forms the corner of the unusually named Teapot Street, and nearby Sheepwash Lane reminds visitors of bygone farm days.

Hanging Langford, Steeple Langford and Little Langford straddle both sides of the river and then at Serrington, just before Stapleford, the Wylye is swelled by the little Till, a small stream travelling southwards from beyond Shrewton, pretty much in the middle of Salisbury Plain. Tilshead, further north, would seem the more obvious choice for the stream to start, but no, apprently the name has a quite different derivation.

It was from the downland around Tilshead, however, that commenced the Great Flood of 1841, the 'Aweful Visitation' that overtook the Till valley. For a sudden thaw followed a heavy mid-January snowfall, and downhill swirled the great torrent without warning, gathering strength and depth as it cascaded through

Cottage in the Wylye Valley with chequerwork walls. (G. T.)

farmland and villages, sweeping away people and animals, cottages, outbuildings, trees and chalky debris.

It happened in the five o'clock gloom of the winter evening, so that most of the country folk had not yet retired to their beds, or the disaster would surely have been greater, but even so, many lives were lost, together with precious livestock and dwellings.

A plaque commemorates the rebuilding of a row of cottages 'Subscribed to Repair the Losses Sustained by The Poor of This and Five Neighbouring Parishes in the Great Flood of 1841'. A local rector wrote a dramatic account which he published to help with the appeal fund.

Beside the Till stands another tiny lock-up similar to the one at Heytesbury, built in 1727 in beehive shape, its interior dark and cold with one small barred window, a salutary experience for the town's troublemakers to ponder their sins in chilly isolation.

The stream lazes through the fields to Winterbourne Stoke, bisected by the rushing A303, and on to Berwick St. James a long village with terraced houses and narrow pavements.

The old church is small and comfortable, with a Norman doorway, and congregations contemplate the wide pointed chancel arch fashioned in the 13th century, and coloured glass in the lancets above the altar.

Stapleford's church is a strong flint building above pretty cottages of whitewash and thatch, and flint and brick chequering. Inside, handsomely carved Norman arches rest on stout round pillars, banded alternately in stone of white and soft green.

The mound near to the church is all that is left of a castle believed to have been built for Waleran, who hunted with William in his New Forest, and may have been a Ranger there.

The short journey of the Till is nearly over as it passes under Pelican Bridge on the main road from Salisbury to Warminster, and between Riverside Garage and the long whitewashed and stone Pelican Inn with its old beams, to join the Wylye in the fields beyond. It is a full grown river now, the Wylye, keeping company with the

The Till at Shrewton with beehive lock-up. (N.O'D.)

lane that leads to Wishford Magna, Great Wishford, spread into quite a large community.

It seems to have been a charitable village always. Sir Richard Grobham, who has a monument in the church, built a row of almshouses in 1628, Grobham Cottages, with quaintly steep-sloping rooves and little mullioned windows, for 'four poor people and one housekeeper'; and in 1722, Sir Richard Howe founded the adjacent school for a basic education to be given to forty pupils, '20 poor boys and 20 poor girls', both buildings still of great benefit to the village.

The church stands opposite them, with the history of Wishford within its walls. The Bonham family inherited the manor in 1278, and there is a tale to tell of the 15th century Sir Thomas. When twins were delivered to his young wife, he, for reasons of his own, took himself off on a pilgrimage to the Holy Land and remained away for seven years. Within a year of returning to the bosom of a family who scarcely remembered him, his long-suffering wife presented him with septuplets. They were all carried to the church for baptism in a charger, or large dish.

'The oldest known manual fire engine' by Richard Newsham, is exhibited in the church, a tiny red toytown affair, little more than a box on solid wheels with four small hoses, purchased by the churchwardens in 1728 for the sum of £33.3s.0d. Perhaps it was better than nothing, but in the face of a fierce blaze it would have been tragically inadequate.

Great Wishford's big day is May 29th, Oak Apple Day, when there is a day-long shindig over ancient rights, though it was on March 15th in 1603 that a meeting was held in Grovely Forest bordering the south of the village, setting out the rights of the people on the collection of free firewood.

The event begins early in the morning with a noisy awakening for slackers, fancy-dressing-up and a procession, and a trip to the cathedral, with dancing and much brandishing of greenery from the forest, and the traditional chant of 'Grovely, Grovely, Grovely and all Grovely', followed by feasting and carnival; an Oak Apple Club was formed in 1892 to 'enforce' the perpetuity of the custom.

Stoford, South Newton and Chilhampton all overlook the river across the fields, and then road and river meet together at Wilton.

An old town, Wilton, perhaps even before the Saxons were there. Important too, since it gave the county its name; Wiltunscir, shire round Wiltun, town of the Wiley. And a capital of sorts, with a palace, for in 838, just a year before he died, the West Saxon King Egbert was acknowledged at 'the royal borough of Wilton' as 'overlord of all English kingdoms', though it was a flimsy claim.

Egbert founded a Benedictine nunnery there, later encouraged by Alfred, for years the area's all important Abbey. It is said that when the bishop, weary of bickering, left Old Sarum to build a new cathedral, he approached the abbess with a view to siting it on her land, but she refused, a waspish decision that cost Wilton its place as Wiltshire's 'capital' and yielded it to Salisbury.

At the dissolution, Wilton went the way of all abbeys, and its stone was taken for the building of a great house for the estate's new owner, Sir William Herbert, first Earl of Pembroke. Hans Holbein was to design it, and the ground plan is mostly his work, but he died long before it was completed and within a hundred years the house was destroyed by fire. A lovely porch of his survives, a garden feature now.

Inigo Jones built the new mansion with his son-in-law, John Webb, and all the magnificence and splendour and treasures can now be seen by everyone, together with 'Fun for all the family' by the simple expedient of paying at the door. There is indeed, much worth seeing.

The entrance itself is impressive, a tree-lined driveway leading to the Triumphal Arch topped by the equestrian statue of Marcus Aurelius, built in the 18th century by Sir William Chambers.

Wilton House was always a favourite with guests. Queen Elizabeth took her court there in 1573, and James I reckoned it was 'the finest House in the land', which must have piqued him a little; still, he enjoyed his visits, and it is said that the first performance of 'As You Like It' was given there for him, possibly in the presence of the bard himself.

Sir Philip Sidney married the second earl's sister, Mary, in 1577, and there wrote his book 'Arcadia' which seems appropriate, enjoying the company of the Elizabethan in-crowd of literature, Edmund Spenser, Christopher Marlowe, and later Ben Jonson.

Charles I regularly escaped the heat of London's putrid streets for summer holidays in Wilton's green freshness, and nearer our own time is the inspiration Winston Churchill found in the peaceful grounds for his painting; there too, the planning took place for the fateful D-Day, when the Southern Command had its headquarters at Wilton House.

The United Kingdom Land Forces still have their headquarters in the town, one of ten Divisions.

But Wilton is famous not only for its great house; its carpets are appreciated worldwide, and the Pembroke family had more than one hand in that too. Not at the beginning, for sheep have always grazed the downs of Wiltshire, and the Wylye valley was a centre for the medieval wool trade.

An industry had developed on the outskirts of the town making woollen cloth, and Wylye water was used in the washing and dyeing of the wool, and the finishing of the cloth. The oldest weaving sheds of these times are still in use, exhibiting the old ways to visitors. Unprofessional competition challenged the home-industry, a problem which was put before the king, and in 1699, William III responded by granting a charter to 'The Clothiers and Weavers of Wilton'.

By this time the resourceful weavers had found a way to use the coarse wool unsuitable for cloth, producing a cheap form of drugget as an early floor covering. This development coincided with the eighth earl's travels in Europe, where he saw carpets of superior quality unmatched in England.

Huguenots in France at that time were suffering severe persecution for their faith, and the earl smuggled two skilled weavers across the Channel, bringing them to Wilton where they were to teach their craft to local men; a special loom was patented in 1741, and cut-pile carpets were on the English market for the first time.

In 1828, after the 'rival' company in Axminster was virtually put out of business by fire, their equipment was bought by the Wilton Factory, since when both Axminster and Wilton carpets have been made there.

In 1944, though it continued to trade at Wilton, the company was bought by the Solent Carpet factory in Southampton, itself no longer in business, though premises at Romsey are still in operation.

Wilton House

42

Wilton Royal Carpet Factory. (N. O'D.)

The Wylye runs through the factory in two streams and is vital to the industry, but now wool comes in great 400lb bales from Australia and Ireland, is spun with 20% of nylon, scoured and washed in long vats; and then the hardy yarn is hung on poles, dipped into cold dye and boiled.

Woolsheds resound with an unbelievable clatter, and weaving machines hold a maze of weft threads from 8,000 bobbins for a 40 feet carpet width, a giant 'cat's cradle' taking days to set up.

Wilton and Axminster carpets give comfort in royal residences, stately houses and smaller homes throughout the world, and are tramped over by countless feet in airports, hotels, liners, theatres, clubs, businesses and High Street shops. The largest, in 1987, was an Axminster woven especially for a Dallas ballroom, when fifteen pieces each 36 × 42 feet were shipped to Texas and there sewn together by hand, three-quarters of an acre in total.

Having finished its commercial duty, the Wylye flows on into the town, sparkling through the green on pleasure bent and under the road to the grounds of Wilton House, where it joins with the River Nadder for their last few miles to Salisbury.

The River Nadder

Helpful local people explaining where the Nadder starts, bring the Avon-phrase 'it dussent rise nowhere' to mind; everyone seems to have a different idea of the source, and indeed the river does gather itself together from a variety of springs spread like splayed fingers between two main sources north of Shaftesbury.

The northernmost brook rises in Wincombe Park, home for a time of the well-loved historian Sir Arthur Bryant, who died at Salisbury in 1985, while the lower stream, the Don, comes up from beyond Donhead St. Andrew and St. Mary to join the sister stream.

Just south of the little river lies Wardour, not a village but a handful of dwellings large and small and three major landmarks.

The oldest by far is Wardour Castle, a romantic ruin in wide, wooded parkland above a tranquil lake. A clutch of signposts directs visitors through winding lanes, for the castle is open to callers for much of the year.

Wardour Castle. (N.O'D.)

First mention of Wardour was found in a document of the late 9th century, and was perhaps one of the great Alfred's royal manors. At the time of Domesday the land belonged to Wilton Abbey and owners can be traced from that date.

John, the first Lord Lovel lived there in 1393 and King Richard II granted his request to be allowed to fortify the house, giving it the castellated appearance seen today. Lord Lovel campaigned in France during the Hundred Years War, and his appreciation of French architectural style influenced his new design, rare in being hexagonal. The castle changed hands during the turmoil of the Wars of the Roses, and no one family has lived there for any length of time.

It was bought by Sir Thomas Arundell from Cornwall in 1547, forfeited to the Crown and repurchased in 1570 when it was modernised; but the Civil War left few noble houses unscathed, and Wardour was to suffer extensive damage.

The second Lord Arundell raised a Regiment of Horse and in the spring of 1643 rode northward to join the king's army at Oxford, an opportunity grasped by the Parliamentarian commander, Sir Edward Hungerford, to attack the stronghold.

He offered the elderly Blanche, Lady Arundell, safe conduct if she vacated the castle peacefully, but the redoubtable lady was made of sterner stuff, and her answer was to gather the twenty-five men of her staff in a spirited defence of her home against 1300 besieging troops, while she joined the maids who were recruited to refuel the muskets.

For eight days they held out, but the soldiers threatened to set off mines and the household surrendered. There was another blow in store for Blanche, for Lord Arundell was killed at Oxford just two weeks later.

Legend has it that during the summer the Royalists smuggled in a young spy to sabotage the guns and poison the well, but he was caught and confessed his role.

The following year it was the turn of the king's men to besiege Wardour; they regained possession, but a third of the building was blown away when mines were set off accidentally; the structure was beyond practical repair and abandoned as a home for family occupation.

When Charles II was restored to the monarchy a 'small' Wardour House was built near to the castle, providing more comfortable quarters for the family.

A new Wardour Castle in the form of a grand Palladian mansion was designed for the eighth Lord Arundell by James Paine, and built in 1776 a mile or so away from the ruin, a huge central block with two wings, the largest and most extravagant Georgian house in Wiltshire, although Christopher Hussey wrote of it, 'No building could be less open to the charge of pretentiousness. It is chastity itself.'

A graceful double curved staircase in the magnificent central hall measures nearly fifty feet in diameter, with elegantly wrought balustrades, beneath a most beautiful carved and glassed dome supported by eight Corinthian columns.

The house contains many treasures of architecture, furniture and art, including several portraits of the Arundell family, one of which is an Angelica Kauffman copy of the gallant Blanche, by Van Dyck.

The religious difficulties of the time caused catholics no small problem, and a chapel was built inconspicuously into the house where it could be easily disguised. After lavish redecoration, it is reckoned to be 'one of the most beautiful and impressive catholic churches in the country', and now serves the neighbourhood's catholic community.

A book has been compiled by Barry Williamson, an amateur historian, recording the fascinating reminiscences of staff and friends of the Arundell family early this century, and among many interesting titbits, we learn that the kitchen of the new castle 'was so enormous that one of the family had her first riding lessons around the kitchen table'.

The house was occupied until 1944, when the sixteenth Lord Arundell died without an heir and the estate was broken up. The mansion was until recently Cranborne Chase School for girls.

The old castle had earlier been left to the nation and is now in the care of English Heritage. Visitors can picnic in extensive grounds and wander over the remains of three levels, exploring a second floor open to the sky, a first floor hall which was used for daily living, with a kitchen, buttery, withdrawing chambers, solar and chapel, the ground floor cellars, storerooms and porter's lodge, and see the well featured in the Civil War story; they can also ponder over the whimsical grotto built into a high bank facing the castle, and occasionally, enjoy imaginative social events staged within the old walls.

On through the varied scenery of the Vale of Wardour winds the Nadder, a different character from the Wylye valley, no longer chalk-based.

At the small town of Tisbury, it skirts the churchyard wall of St. John the Baptist, a large and handsome building. The parents of Rudyard Kipling retired to Tisbury after service in India, and now lie beneath flat gravestones near the south-east corner, Alice, who died in 1910, and John Lockwood Kipling, following a year later.

On the opposite side, the famous Tisbury yew stands guardian by the main gate, reputed to be a thousand years old. Apocryphal or not, it is certainly an ancient tree, not very tall, but with an enormous spread, its splayed trunk measuring thirty-one feet in circumference, growing round a huge boulder, itself twelve feet or so in height and of great girth, an amazing spectacle.

The interior of this well-loved church presents a bit of a piece-meal appearance, so much of interest it has to offer visitors.

Across the eastern churchyard wall in the 1700s, the cheerless workhouse gave shelter to the poor of the area, listed in a sad poem by the Rev. George Crabbe as orphans, aged childless parents, heartbroken matrons, 'forsaken wives, and mothers never wed', dejected widows, the crippled, lame, blind, idiot and madman; a sorry lot, existing in dreadful conditions, their diet bread and cheese for three days a week, interspersed with soup and bread on one day, and bacon and potatoes the other two, and the joy of a suet dumpling on Sundays.

After a Commission reported its findings in 1862, efforts were made at improvement; a new workhouse was opened six years later, and the old building sold to local man Archibald Beckett, who turned it into a brewery, re-built after a fire in 1885.

Mr. Beckett's name still spans the entrance, and it is still a brewery though after several changes of use, the Wiltshire Brewery, specialising in traditional brews with descriptive names, Stonehenge Best Bitter,

Medieval Barn, Place House, Tisbury. (G.T.)

Olde Grumble, Old Devil, and their own unique alcoholic ginger beer. Perhaps the river and the springs that feed it were used in Mr. Beckett's beer, but in these purity-conscious days it takes no part in the industry.

Travelling westwards, the Nadder cuts through the fields of Place Farm, an arrangement of wonderfully atmospheric buildings of medieval age. The archway through an impressive gatehouse shows a tantalising glimpse of lawns and flower beds, and a very satisfying stone house. Beside it, a herd of cattle in the yard, bordered by a great buttressed barn, the largest in England, nearly 200 feet long and 32 feet wide, with 'chapel' porches, pigeons and collared doves sunning themselves on the wide expanse of thatched roof, supported inside by an intricate sculpture of great rough beams; a humble barn only, and used as such, but of enormous grandeur.

The farm was once a grange, part of Shaftesbury Abbey, but habitation goes much farther back than that. Sir Richard Colt Hoare, researching the area in the 1820s, wrote of a Stonehenge-like circle in one of its fields, with upright sarsen stones within a ditch and bank, reckoned to have been erected about 3000 years ago.

At least three of the giant slabs were arbitrarily removed in 1792 by Lord Arundell, owner of the land, for the grotto at his Wardour castle, built by Joseph Lane who specialised in such constructions. The field, on the Chicksgrove road, is known still as Lost Stone field.

A single-arch hump-bridge of aged stone leads to the straggling village, guinea-fowl and sheep ranging across the fields, and a secretive tree-creeper running up the black-coned alders, slender bill picking out insects hidden in the bark.

At Chicksgrove too, was a quarry worked before Roman soldiers tramped the valley; and a quarry there is now, just across the lane, an open quarry yielding an attractive honey coloured stone which weathers well and is much in demand locally for building, garden walls and rockeries. It also provides the stone used in the long-term renovation of Salisbury Cathedral, for it comes from the same bed as the better known Chilmark Quarry nearby, which provided so much material for buildings and sculptures of the area, and from which the cathedral took 50,000 tons for its construction in the 13th century.

Behind the quarry is a copse and a pond, fed from a pipe near the railway bridge with clear fresh water from the Nadder, which combination of woodland and water, the owner hopes to develop into a quiet sanctuary for wild life.

Chicksgrove's 'local' is the Compasses Inn, once a smuggler's haunt, gained by a stone-flagged path past Plum Cottage. Its oldest parts are 15th century or perhaps earlier, the bar a dark cavern with stone floor, candle lit in the evenings, with marbles, bar skittles, shove-halfpenny, darts, and other old games available to customers. There are pots and pans of copper and iron, a collection of jugs and mugs hanging from the low beams, and high-backed settles, in the corner of one of which a tabby cat snoozes before a huge log fire.

Perhaps long-ago farmhands edged respectfully back from the warmth so that Sir John Davies could sit before that same fireplace, for in the 16th century, Chicksgrove had its own celebrity; Sir John, as well as writing poetry, was Attorney-General for Ireland. He was called to the bar in 1595, but disbarred a couple of years later for a 'grave breach of discipline', during which, in the Temple dining-room, 'attended by two men with swords, he pulled a cudgel from under his gown and broke it over a colleague's head'! But his transgression was forgiven, and he was reinstated in 1601.

Sutton Mandeville hides at the end of a lane between steep banks, its church well hidden among the trees, and then the Nadder creeps quietly through the Vale fed by small streams, particularly pretty at Teffont Evias and Teffont Magna.

And then it is on to Dinton, a large village with a sturdy church on a mound, and several noble mansions and manors.

Hyde House is one, at Little Clarendon, for Edward Hyde was born at Dinton, the third son of a modest landowner; he it was who studied well and became Charles II's Lord Chancellor, later first Earl of Clarendon, and whose nephew's widow protected the king at Heale House at Woodford.

There is Lawes Cottage, too, wherein lived Thomas Lawe, vicar-choral at Salisbury, and his family. William and Henry both inherited their father's musical ability and became composers, but the Civil War affected this family as all others, and William was killed in battle at Chester in 1645; Henry was a Gentleman of King Charles I's Chapel Royal, and one of the king's musicians, but there was no place for these Court positions in wartime, and he 'betook himself to the teaching of ladies to sing', his 'irreproachable life and gentlemanly deportment' making him ideal for this occupation.

Henry Lawe was one of the most important song-writers of the 17th century, composing sacred and secular music, and more than four hundred of his songs have survived. He was a friend of John Milton, and wrote the music for his masque of 'Comus', and to Henry, Milton dedicated a sonnet 'to Mr. H. Lawes on his Aires'.

In the middle of green parkland stands Philipps House, designed in 1816, with an imposing Ionic portico, and within, a lofty hall and graceful staircase; the mansion is now leased to the Young Women's Christian Association and used as a conference centre.

After the rather dull Barford St. Martin comes the suburb of Ditchampton where until 1951 lived A. G. Street, farmer, writer and broadcaster, his daughter Pamela a writer also, about the Wiltshire they both loved.

Palladian Bridge, Wilton House. (G. T.)

The river flows under a many arched bridge beside the long village of Burcombe, with the Ship Inn on its banks and Saxon long and short work in the church walls, past Bulbridge and into the peaceful grounds of Wilton House, where a handsome Palladian bridge, designed by Roger Morris, was built over the slow-moving Nadder.

Before it reaches the main A3094, the Nadder is joined by the Wylye, and together they head for the cathedral city, calling on the way at Quidhampton with its pretentiously quaint 'Model Farm' of fancy-stonework, and including an elaborate dovecote, all for the amusement of a 19th-century Russian-born Countess of Pembroke.

It calls also at Bemerton, where the Earl of Pembroke's cousin, George Herbert, was rector for three short years, from 1630 until he died of consumption in 1633 at the too-early age of forty; a beautiful window honours him in the north choir aisle of the cathedral, and he is figured, too, in the west window of his own small church.

A dear and good man, George Herbert was a learned scholar and seemed to be destined for a position of worldly power, but he settled instead for the work of a parish priest in this small village near to his kinsmen at Wilton. He wrote a good deal of poetry, and his works are on display at the church he served and where he was so well-loved. His verses are sung in hymns familiar to congregations everywhere, and include the lines which have provided the inspiration for many a sermon:

> 'A man that looks on glass
> On it may stay his eye;
> Or if he pleaseth, thro' it pass
> And then the heaven espy.'

A pleasant walk, no doubt followed sometimes by the gentle rector, would have taken him to the Old Mill at West Harnham, older than Salisbury itself, a picturesque and tranquil corner of the Nadder on the southern side of the Cathedral Close.

John Constable was a frequent visitor to Salisbury during the 1820s, for his close friend, John Fisher, was Archdeacon there, and he made several sketches and drawings whilst strolling in the area. The view of the cathedral across these water meadows was a particular favourite, and he made a pencil drawing, later translated on to canvas, which he called 'The Rainbow', now in a private collection.

The Old Mill, West Harnham. (N.O'D.)

The Bishop of Salisbury, uncle of the Archdeacon, made use of his nephew's friendship with the painter, and commissioned a picture of the cathedral from a similar angle; the bishop and his wife appear in the corner. For many throughout the world, Constable's paintings of the cathedral are all they will ever know of Salisbury.

The Old Mill may have been built as early as 1135, its decorative squares of flints wonderfully matched, and during the construction of the cathedral after the closure of Old Sarum, was used to house the church artefacts.

It has served several purposes, and was not converted into a water mill until the mid-1500s, in which use it continued until 1931. It is a restaurant now with a full range of menus and specialising in connoisseur coffees with liqueur and a topping of fresh cream.

A glass-topped counter enables customers to peer down into the gloom and see the frothing water gushing through a narrow channel beneath the mill.

And then visitors can tread the Town Path and Long Bridge as Constable did, across the water-meadows to the Cathedral Close, and by that most pleasant of routes, enter the great city of Salisbury.

Opposite: The Cathedral overlooking the Close.

Salisbury to Downton (and Ebble)

For miles around, and on all the approach roads to Salisbury, the beautiful spire is the focus of every view, 404 feet high, unmatched in Great Britain and surpassed in Europe only by the cathedral of Ulm, on the banks of the Danube in Germany; even there, it is the building which is more vast and high, and the spire alone, of Salisbury, is the taller.

The city grew around the cathedral, begun in 1220 by Bishop Poore from Old Sarum after his problems there, and consecrated just thirty-eight years later, although building continued well into the next century.

The vision of the men who designed such a masterpiece can only be marvelled at, and those who translated the vision into stone and glass, no less.

In the north transept is set out an imaginative model, fascinating and detailed, which gives an idea of the construction site, a township in itself with its carpenter's shop, which handled 3500 tons of oak from forests of the south, the glazier and the forge; stables for the horses and oxen which hauled the heavy materials, the mason's workshop in which was shaped and sculpted 50,000 tons of white Chilmark stone and 15,000 tons of dark Purbeck marble, carried up the Avon on barges from Worth Matravers near Poole, and the limekiln where limestone was heated and mixed with sand and water from the river to make mortar.

There was the hut where each man's wage was counted out and handed over, and a tavern in which to spend it when the long day's toil was finished. Building sites have always been dangerous places, and accidents and sickness took their toll; men died, and were buried in the corner graveyard there.

The model brings an exciting reality to the creation of these great medieval cathedrals, but there still remains the deep sense of wonder at the grace and elegance of the clustered pillars and the magnificence of the vaulting above them, all wrought by man; no practical explanation can diminish that miracle.

Opposite: The Nave.

But even miracles sometimes require hard cash to survive, and in this same transept is set out an ambitious exhibition for the Spire Appeal, for millions of pounds are needed to restore the crumbling stonework of this truly lovely cathedral.

Sarum's first bishop, Osmund, died in 1099, his shrine a feature of the nave; elsewhere lies a stone lid, reputed to be from his coffin, brought down from the old cathedral on the hill. In the nave too, stands a clock of 1386, the oldest in England and restored in 1956 to full working order.

Another treasure, displayed with other rare books and manuscripts in the Chapter House, is the Magna Carta, the original document that meant so much to the people of England in 1215, brought to Salisbury by a half-brother of King John.

The peaceful cloisters are the oldest in England, but a cathedral is a living building, and in the east, startlingly deep cobalt-blue glass in the five lancets of the Trinity Chapel, was the work in 1980 of a French master glazier.

The river which borders the Close, flowing through the water-meadows, has already seen the commercial city, passing behind the Playhouse and the fine shopping centre set out to the north of the cathedral. 'Capital of the Avon' Salisbury may be, but not the county town, which honour falls to Trowbridge near the Somerset border.

The medieval streets contain the four entrance gateways to the city, ancient churches, and the houses, shops and inns that have served the customers of centuries with names that match the beams and half-timbers, steep rooves and peep-windows — the Pheasant Hotel, and Haunch of Venison, the Antelope, Griffin and Three Swans.

Traders still set up their stalls in the Market Place, where the craftsmen and countryfolk of six hundred years have brought their wares and produce for sale, its focal point the ornate Poultry Cross, which has sheltered stallholders from the Wiltshire weather since at least 1335.

In the Market Place, so it is said, by Blue Boar Row, the executioner caught up with the wily 2nd Duke of Buckingham in 1483, beheaded for treachery on the orders of Richard III, and arguably the cause of many of that young man's problems.

The Poultry Cross, Salisbury. (G. T.)

The House of John a'Port was built in 1425 for a merchant grown rich in the lucrative wool trade, and the name of the larger-than-life mayor a generation later, lives on in his home — Ye Halle of John Halle.

Within the Close too, are lovely, mellow old houses, each with a long and dignified history, some of them open to visitors who may share their secrets.

With all this wonderful atmosphere of ages, the architecture, the green Close, and the deep river lazing through, the town has always attracted painters, musicians and writers.

In his autobiography, Anthony Trollope told readers that the idea for his novel 'The Warden' came to him on a visit to Salisbury, although the plot was based on happenings at the similar establishment at St. Cross, Winchester. He had a particular fondness for this slim book, the first of the six 'Barsetshire Chronicles', not least perhaps, because it was his first to be a financial success, for he was forty when it was published in 1855 and his work had not until then achieved public acclaim.

The charming, but rather sad story concerns an almshouse, Hiram's Hospital, and although the author was always scrupulously indefinite about his cathedral location, who, familiar with St. Nicholas' Hospital at East Harnham, could fail to see it in Trollope's description: 'Hiram's Hospital, as the retreat is called, is a picturesque building enough, and shows the correct taste with which the ecclesiastical architects of those days were imbued. It stands on the banks of the little river, which flows nearly round the cathedral close, being on the side furthest from town . . .'

One of the oldest buildings in Salisbury, St. Nicholas' Hospital was founded by Bishop Poore for the comfort of the poverty-stricken sick, and now its ancient rooms are quiet within the thick arched walls, the stone-flagged passageway cool, and with that inimitable redolence of peaceful age.

A pleasing new complex has been built in the old gardens, and St. Nicholas' is still a happy retirement home for twenty-four residents, the 'master', like Trollope's Septimus Harding, a retired clergyman, the smooth lawns sweeping down to an Avon stream.

In this delightful corner, the river flows under St. Nicholas Road in two branches, with gardens on their banks, summer gardens green and colourful, secluded behind drooping willows and tall rambling roses.

The 14th-century Rose and Crown, half-timbered and low-beamed stands behind a narrow pavement, opposite a row of cottages with skep-like thatched porches supported by two tree-trunks apiece; but the river loops in the other direction, to straighten awhile by the Southampton Road, Churchill Gardens making a most attractive informal park for walking and picnicking, before turning south once more, and getting rather untidy as it splits itself into many separate channels on its way to the coast.

Between the channels sits rural Britford, a village long before Salisbury was built, its first mention found in 670, so many variations of its early name that a derivation is still a subject for discussion.

Eighteenth-century Bridge Farm straddles the river, a narrow lane leading to the church, and to The Moat House, a low castle-like dwelling with attractive window mouldings and water all about it.

St Peter's is tree-shaded, surrounded by open green fields and the river to one side, a large church for the scattered community, with a high nave and a Saxon door on the south side. An unusual gateway offers the comfort of low stone seats on either side, and just beyond, a second gate which stands alone and seems to have no purpose, an oddity, but of such is made up the patchwork of life.

Two shallow recesses in the nave were uncovered during restoration last century, the entrance arches incorporating rare Roman bricks and tiles with a cable pattern entwined with vines, thought to be 9th-century work.

The Jerveys family bought the estate from the Earl of Huntingdon in 1542, and in the north transept a beautifully sculpted 'open book' in marble remembers G. P. Jervoise and his descendants. Opposite, the Parish Chest of about 1450, bears the required three locks of the time, reminiscent of the offertory box in Bishop's Cannings, at the beginning of the Avon story.

'Lord Radnor's pews' take up the entire south transept, his family and servants once regularly attending, but not used now, and in the chancel, the Buckingham Tomb is thought to be the elaborate burial place of the executed second duke, Henry Stafford.

The tall broach steeple of Alderbury church is a landmark across the river, Alderbury, whose Green Dragon found favour with Charles Dickens; he stayed there for a while, gathering material for one of his lighter novels, Martin Chuzzlewit, and changing the name somewhat unimaginatively to the Blue Dragon — 'a common, paltry, low-minded, clodhopping, pipe-smoking ale-house' one of his characters called it, but another had a more charitable view — ' . . . this noble Dragon, which . . . has my good word and my good wish to the day of my death.'

Part brick and half-timbered, part cream-washed, with a steep roof, the Green Dragon claims that its main bar was the 'hall-house' of the 12th-century Ivychurch Priory, long since demolished; beneath a tiled roof, a handsome, ivy-covered horse-trough stands by the roadside, constructed from 'columns and capitals from the cloisters' of the Priory.

The next few miles of land around the Avon belong to the Earl of Radnor of Longford Castle, an unusual triangular building of elaborate design with round turrets, all patterned in stone and flint, and long lawns beside the river.

It replaced a smaller manor-house belonging to Sir Thomas Gorges, who in 1584, married Helena, a widowed marchioness, maid of honour to Queen Elizabeth. Their new home was hugely expensive to build, and funds were insufficient to meet the cost; but Sir Thomas held the post of Governor of Hurst Castle on the Hampshire coast, and providentially, one of the galleons of the Spanish Armada foundered within its jurisdiction.

Now, did the resourceful couple know what the ship carried, or did they take a gamble? However it was, Lady Gorges asked the Queen if they might claim the wreck, and when the vessel was found to be loaded with silver bars, the revenue more than covered the completion of their extravagant new home. Sir Philip Sidney, writing his 'Arcadia' at Wilton, was an early and admiring visitor, and based his 'Castle of Amphialus' on Longford.

Sir Thomas and his lady are buried in the cathedral's North Choir Aisle, a tall monument erected to them.

In 1717, the Bouverie family bought the estate, and inevitably changes have been made. The eighth earl values his privacy, and the castle is well secluded.

On a westward slope was built Trafalgar House in 1814, a brick mansion given as a somewhat contentious tribute to the late sea-hero, for it was Nelson's brother who benefited from the grand gesture, and he and Horatio had not always lived in harmony.

Much of the land here is private property, and uninvited callers are not welcome, but there are public footpaths where ramblers can enjoy a peaceful stroll among the riverside glory, past fragrant pink and white chestnut spikes, remote houses with tumbles of honeysuckle over their walls, and a sleeping Rip Van Winkle church, knee-deep in cow-parsley and goose-grass; pigeons clatter from thick woodlands across lush meadows to the tree-crowned hills beyond; and there is birdsong, and the cawing of rooks as they, like the grey herons, patch up their homes for the new season; and just occasionally, if the East Anglian winter is too severe, a shy brown bittern may visit, though the casual rambler would be lucky to see it.

By the river, bright kingcups have given way to the soft, bee-full fluff of meadowsweet, plank bridges cross various streams where swallows dip and swoop, and there is the sound of water falling over the weir. For this is fishermen's country, from Salisbury down to the sea, and more controversially to some, fish-farming country.

This is the Avon of the roach and the dace, trout and salmon, grayling, pike and chub, and in the autumn, eels; it all provides a healthy diet for the rare otters that shimmy through the tall grass and steal all the best fish, but they are more welcome than the predatory mink, vicious and aggressive, killing without reason.

At the southern end of the estate, the Avon's last major tributary from the west joins with the mainstream, the little Ebble, from Berwick St. John out towards Shaftesbury.

When other roads are dry, water trickles over the surface of farm lanes beyond Berwick St. John, gathering itself together under a bank starred with bright enamelled celandines and shaggy dandelions, an unpretentious infancy for the lazy River Ebble.

A narrow streamside road is bordered by a terrace of grey stone cottages with pretty names, the front room of one of them serving as the village post-office; and if the post-van meets a tractor, well, someone has to give way, for the single lane does not cater for them both.

The rural village does boast a bus service, and at the cross-roads, passengers wait comfortably in a stout stone bus shelter with three arches.

There is a lot of grey stone in the Ebble Valley and the hills are gently rounded Dorset-like, for only a ridge separates the two counties.

On one of those hills, early in the 18th century, the Reverend John Gane stayed too late one winter's night and lost his bearings, a fright not easily forgotten by a clerical gentleman; for the sake of others who might find themselves in similar distress, he left a legacy for the church bell to be tolled at eight o'clock each winter's eve, that any strays may be guided to the village, a practice only recently discontinued.

Goldfinches squabble during communal bathing in the lane-side puddles of Alvediston, leafy lanes that may have been trodden by descendants of Sir Gowain, one of Arthur's Knights of the Round Table, for the estate once belonged to the Gawen family, from 1377; another version of the name, Gawain, occurs elsewhere in the valley, all of which has been held to support an interesting possibility.

The handsome Norrington Manor, part medieval, part Elizabethan, was home to the Wyndham family who bought the estate from the Gawens in 1658, and memories of both dynasties are in the church.

At Ebbesbourne Wake the stream flows beside the lane, with sheep in the fields and hedge-sparrows stealing tags of wool caught on fences to make their nests snug, sounds of wood-cutting, and cows leaving muddy cloven footprints at the meadow's edge. A sturdy chapel at the village cross-roads faces the tall-towered church, primroses massing wild in its sloping grounds.

The narrow stream trickles through the fields of Fifield Bavant, overlooked by one of the country's smallest churches, perched rather austerely on a knoll, its simple outline without embellishment, tiny bell turret above the door at the west end.

No road leads to St. Martin's, for farmland surrounds the hillock; but the wide gates over concrete hard-standing are all ajar, and worshippers file through the farmyard and up the narrow, stony footpath.

Fifield Bavant Church approach through farmyard. (N.O'D.)

Just thirty-five chairs are set out within these 13th-century flint and stone walls, for it measures but 35 feet by 14 feet. Several small windows let in shafts of sunlight, the slit of one original lancet on the north side; the font is probably a hundred years older, with deep scallops patterning the rim.

Energetic parishioners enjoy the Rogationtide walk, which, explains a notice, will start at Ebbesbourne Vicarage, going on to Alvediston and Norrington, to the Herepath, round Chiselbury Rings and Fovant Badges, and back to Fifield for, assuredly, a most welcome tea, before joining together for the lovely old prayers of Evensong.

A fair distance, for the Fovant Badges are a series of intricate carvings, Regimental Badges cut by soldiers of the First World War into the hills separating the Ebble Valley from the Nadder, and facing the A30 road from Shaftesbury to Salisbury, where a lay-by has been built so that travellers can pull in and admire safely, with a telescope for even better viewing.

By the time the Ebble gets to Broad Chalke, largest village in the valley, it has widened and deepened, flowing beside the road with sinuous grey shadows weaving between the green weed and water-mint, coots and white farm ducks foraging.

Students of Wiltshire's history owe a great debt to the county's first antiquarian, John Aubrey, whose detailed work has been the basis for years of subsequent writings. He lived at Broad Chalke in the 17th century, serving as warden in the big church that was old even then. He was a farmer too, not averse to experimenting with new ways as well as delving into the old. He was proud of the trout in his stretch of the river, but for a change 'did putt in craw-fish, but they would not live there'. Too cold, he reckoned.

This is water-cress country, green beds set out between streamlets and bridges, fed by springs of the Ebble around Stoke Farthing, Croucheston, Bishopstone.

Bishops of Winchester used to own Bishopstone, its 14th century church beyond the village; and its neighbour, Stratford Tony, was among land given to Ralf Toni, a Norman soldier who held the important position of standard bearer to William, during the fateful Battle of Hastings. But the Romans knew the road long before William, using the ford across the Ebble on their journeys to and from Sarum.

Salisbury Race Course lies on the downland between the Ebble and the Nadder, Netherhampton on the north edge, Coombe Bissett to the south, and a 'new' 18th century bridge crosses the river, replacing the medieval Packhorse Bridge nearby.

The road through Homington leads on to Odstock, where a collection of unprepossessing buildings and assorted huts greet the visitor to Odstock Hospital; to the casual eye the clutter of temporary and permanent wards looks unco-ordinated, but its unrivalled reputation for the treatment of burns has never been in doubt.

The need for a hospital to provide emergency medical services in 1944, for casualties from the invasion of Europe, brought about the building of Odstock, but its current facilities provide a range of services — orthopaedic, maternity, medical, children's and elderly care, with a Spinal Treatment Centre, and a special unit for burns, plastic surgery and maxillo facial services, where features and jawbones shattered by tragedy are rebuilt with painstaking dedication and skill.

A £26 million project is underway for a new building which will enlarge its own facilities and take over the needs of the Infirmary at Salisbury, planned for closure in the next few years.

The hospital is well away from the river and the village, whose grave-yard holds the bones of a gypsy, the main character in a strange tale from the turn of the century.

The church door, which has a steep step down into the gloom to catch the unwary, is never locked, a tradition arising from a powerful gypsy curse after quiet Joshua Scamp had been tried and hanged for theft; the ne'er-do-well husband of his daughter was the real culprit, but for her sake he kept silent and paid with his life.

On each anniversary of his funeral, gypsies gathered at Odstock in his memory, but like many such affairs, especially where they take place near to licensed premises, it all began to get out of hand; ill-will was generated, and feelings were bruised when the church door was locked against them. The gypsy queen was loud in her curses of individuals, a rumpus heard at the next village of Nunton. But as the months passed, all the curses in turn came true, death and misfortune striking each man named, including he who had locked the church door 'who would not be preaching by the next twelvemonth'.

Two men since have locked the door, by accident and bravado, and both died within the year; discretion was held to be the better part of valour and the door-key was thrown into the Ebble. And Odstock church is never locked. Ralph Whitlock researched the story thoroughly, and has written about it at length, including a radio play, bringing the tale to a wide audience.

And so the Ebble is swallowed into the Avon at Bodenham, another attractive village, comfortably away from the Salibury to Ringwood road, ending in a riverside lane with leafy trees arched overhead.

Charlton, too, favours the river rather than the road, and from the southern end starts a mile and a half footpath to Downton, used only by the hardy when a biting wind sweeps across the open fields from the east, but a delight on balmy days to walk through buttercup meadows under a blue sky, the pinnacled tower of Downton's church in the distance and the wide river between.

The path leads directly into Downton's main thoroughfare, The Borough, by a railed three-arched bridge.

Further eastward the river disappears under the road again, but this time it is a man-made channel, a mill-race diverted from the main river, a still, tree-shaded haven where it meets the road, a nursery for a new family of colourful, grey wagtails skimming the mirror surface, perfect reflections unmarred by the smallest ripple.

Records show that a tanner worked in the village in 1606, and there is nothing unusual in that, but a tannery at Downton there still is.

The river is important to the business, and an old water wheel, visible from the road, is a loved and integral part of the works. A Ponsett undershot wheel, it fell into disrepair in the early '80s and much effort went into the task of finding just the right parts to restore it. Now, powered solely by the mill-race, it helps to keep the machinery turning.

For more than three hundred years the craft had its ups and downs, and in 1919 the old thatched workshop at the east end of the village street was replaced by a commodious new building, for much space is used in the long process of turning hides into malleable leather. Sadly the optimistic new company failed, and was succeeded ten or so years later by the Downton Tanning Company.

Downton Bridge.

Behind the mellow brick walls with their joyous covering of Virginia creeper, long sheds receive best quality cow hides from selected hide markets all over the country, rough, raw, salted to keep them fresh; and there they are sorted and graded and washed in a great revolving drum before being plunged into a repetitious procession of lime-and-sulphide pits to break down the fibres and loosen the hairs, a lengthy business.

The company takes immense care not to allow its pollution into the sparkling river and has won a Gold Award from the Angling Foundation for the treatment of its potentially damaging effluent.

The hides are hung individually and soaked in vats of tan, a mixture of chalky Avon water — the best — and ground tree bark — birch or mimosa — which permeates the fibres and softens the leather. The emphasis throughout the company is on top quality and the tannery is proud of its international reputation for a fine product.

Two hundred hides a day are dispatched on their long journey into leather, a thousand a week. Weeks of gentle drying are followed by checking, grading, sorting, trimming, the pressing out of any remaining creases and sometimes dyeing.

Thinner qualities are snapped up in bulk by the American market and moulded into tool pouches and gun holsters for slotting on to matching belts. The best quality is sent away for dressing, before being crafted into luxury cases and fine riding tack, and daintiest of all, to London for ballet shoes.

There were many local industries in Downton once, but no other has survived: the making of shoes, lace and paper, brickyards, maltsters, baskets from local osier beds, and straw hats, are all gone now.

The village is one of Wiltshire's oldest communities with an earth work at the eastern end, a Moot House of 1700 opposite the age-old site; it appears in the 7th century records, shown as a gift from a West Saxon king to the Bishops of Winchester.

They used to celebrate a fair there at each end of the year, and the April Cuckoo Fair is still a day of festivity, remembering when 'they opened the Forest Gate and let the cuckoo through'. But the forest is on the other side of the county border, for Downton is the southernmost point of Wiltshire.

Downton to Christchurch

Now, at last, it is indeed the Hampshire Avon, with Charford, North and South, just over the border on old water-meadows, the lane verges frilling with nodding heads of Queen Anne's lace.

Cerdic, the Saxon warrior, and his son Cynric, fought there triumphantly against the Britons in 519; a long time ago, but important in local history, since the victor decided to hang up his sea-boots and settle in his newly-won territory as king of the West Saxons, and established a 'royal' line through Cynric and his grandson in the land which was to become known more generally as Wessex. And since Alfred was a descendant of this same line, and our own monarchy is traced back to Alfred, Charford seems to warrant more than a passing tribute.

The river keeps the road pretty much company on this stretch, with a steep footpath, tree-lined, the banks cheerful with red campion leading up to St. Mary's at Hale; from a little further up the path can be spied the pink-washed mansion of Hale Park, though there is a far more grand avenue-approach from the other side.

The architect, Thomas Archer lived there in the house he designed for himself in 1715; there is a great marble monument to him in the south transept, and he watches, stern-faced, as the organist plays.

Built at the same time as the house, the church is a curious mixture of simplicity and fuss, with simplicity winning, and has a pleasing east window of coloured glass depicting the Good Shepherd.

Both house and church look down on a broad curve of the Avon, and this lovely land is heavily wooded with oak and ash, sycamore, willow, lime and horse-chestnut, loud with birdsong, the cuckoo calling across the river.

No sooner does the road leave Hale than it is in Woodgreen, whose small brick church of St. Boniface is of a newer era, and has a colourful children's corner, joyfully used. The place of worship is spotless, tastefully decorated with red and white azaleas in May, the only old item a heavy bible, its pages tattered through years of loving use.

Next door, the village hall stands on a site presented by Sir Hamilton Hulse of nearby Breamore, and inside, the walls are decorated with

71

large murals of the 'daily doings' of the villagers, pictures painted over eighteen months after the hall was opened in 1930, a point of great interest for successive generations.

Woodgreen nibbles at the edge of the New Forest, the only Avon village to do so, and the ponies that give character to Forest land wander through, grazing on the village green, with charming cottages, 'Ye Olde Shoppe and Post Office' and a rustic bus-shelter around the edge.

One of the major tourist attractions of the area is at Breamore, 'Bremmer' to local folk, on the west of the river. An old mill straddles a gathering of streams where regal swans glide, and on the other side of the bridge a small 'shore-line' attracts young paddlers with nets on sticks; the best they will do is to scoop out a stickleback or a minnow or two from the dark clouds of wriggling shoals, but when you are six, it is enough.

Breamore House is the focus for visitors, a lovely Elizabethan manor of rosy brick, with steep gables and a mass of tall chimneys. It was completed in 1583 for the Dodington family, who lived there for nearly a hundred years, and then passed through marriage, to Robert Greville, Lord Brooke, later created Earl of Warwick.

Sir Edward Hulse bought the estate in 1748, and his family still live there, allowing the public to share parts of the house and its priceless contents.

A maze in the grounds attracts the fun-loving intrepid, with various displays and museums of life in yesteryear — a collection of carriages, livestock and workaday scenes in the form of set pieces.

The church of Breamore is a joy, a Saxon treasure thought to have been built about 980, and an ancient yew by the path cannot be much younger than the church, its rotting trunk and branches making natural wood sculptures, large flints strewn among its roots, a host for colourful fungus, saucer-like scallops of bright saffron, with the somewhat quizzical name of chicken in the wood.

Over the south door, much damaged, is a rare Saxon rood depicting Our Lady and St. John, protected now by a later porch; and seven round-headed windows of the same era remain, doubled-splayed in the character of the time. Round the arch of the south transept are

Breamore House.

Breamore Church. (G. T.)

carved Saxon words, unfamiliar, the text, 'here is made plain the covenant to thee', thought to have been completed around the year 1000.

It is a large, complex and colourful church, with much during its thousand years of parish life to excite the ecclesiologist and casual visitor alike.

Below the Shallows, just south of Breamore Mill, the river sweeps east and west in broad loops with manifold small channels; eastward, it touches the Forest border again and then back to glimpse the road at Lower Burgate, before another turn east takes it through the holiday centre of Sandy Balls at Godshill, a Rose Award-winning park of 120 acres.

Comfortable caravans and chalets wait for visitors, secluded in shady woodland, with rural and recreational facilities, a restaurant, well stocked shop and an indoor swimming pool, plus a nature-reserve, and access to river-fishing, some of these pleasures open to non-residents.

Another turn takes it through the grounds of the Game Conservancy, a member organisation whose aims are to encourage the breeding of gamebirds, animals and fish, and to protect and preserve their habitat, both for the enjoyment of the countryside and for sporting management.

A most graceful bridge of seven pointed arches across the Avon is for travellers from the west the first view of Fordingbridge, with flat green playing-fields to one side of the river, and the old coaching-inn, The George, on its bank, tables at the very edge and plentiful ducks paddling and waddling near to be fed. The inn is proud of its 'renowned cheese selection' and 'varied homecooked fayre'.

The town itself is a jumble of narrow streets, a headache to drivers and tradesmen, but with a comfortably bustling atmosphere.

Two little streams sparkle through Fordingbridge, joining at a bridge by Church Street, the Allen River, turning into Ashford Water beyond Damerham, and a smaller brook from a spring in the direction of Rockbourne, with its detailed remains of an extensive Roman villa.

On the corner, a neat Methodist chapel shines in white stone, with a tiny portico and two smooth pillars, the tower of Fordingbridge church looming behind it with features old and new; above modern plate glass doors on the 15th century porch, a Mass clock, one of three under its roof, the font, 700 years old, and in the Lady chapel, wonderful beams and figures carved by medieval craftsmen from chestnut.

Brooks from the New Forest feed the Avon now, different from the chalk streams, red-brown and stony, with low mossy banks, sometimes holding silvery dace, or the darker loach, and maybe even a small trout. Some are little more than ditches until the rains come, others, small torrents swirling over the fords.

Ditchend Brook comes down from the high heathland of Black Gutter Bottom, entering the Avon just before Bickton. The lane runs beside the river here, placid and slow, bright yellow water-lilies on stout stems jutting above flat round leaves, a water-vole zimmering between them, and purple comfrey thick on the bank.

A pretty village, Bickton, at right-angles between the main road and the river, with thatched rooves and colourful gardens, and at its end, a fishery with a retail shop for fresh river catches.

75

Trout from the Avon go into the Smokery behind Bickton Mill, to be cleaned and brined and hung on rails above slow burning oak sawdust, and fine salmon from Scotland are similarly treated; chicken, turkey and quail, ham, pork and venison smoke for hours above smouldering beech chippings. The finished delicacies are then distributed to the markets of London, as well as to local shops, hotels and restaurants, and the Smokery also undertakes small private orders.

Huckles Brook, which starts out as Latchmore Brook, swirls down from the high ground of Studley Wood and into the mainstream before Harbridge.

Harbridge is reached across a grey-stone bridge at Ibsley, its 19th century grey church with a narrow side turret beside the main tower among the meadows, where flocks of lapwings peck among the farm-fields after hay-making.

Across the road from the weir lies the thatched Old Beams Restaurant, and next door, a rather sad-looking church of faded pink brick and clear diamond-paned windows, almost hidden behind old yews and laurel, St. Martins, one short dark path over-hung with evergreens, old crooked gravestones crusted with golden lichen, and unkempt grass and weed; its doors are locked, but house-martins have found a home among old rafters beneath the north porch tiles.

The largest and longest of the Forest streams, Dockens Water, curls down from Fritham through tall Forest trees, and before it joins the Avon passes by the modest brick mansion of Moyles Court, a preparatory school now, with a well known tragic tale in its history.

For Dame Alice Lisle inherited the house in 1638 and lived there for nearly fifty years, her husband one of the judges at the trial of Charles I.

When in her seventies, she was accused of harbouring two sympathisers of the Monmouth rebellion against James II. She denied knowing of their political views, but was arrested and taken before Judge Jeffreys at the Winchester Assize.

The merciless judge allowed no defence to be prepared, browbeat the jury into convicting her, and sentenced the old lady to death by burning at the stake, the sentence to be carried out within hours.

Dockens Water, near Moyles Court. (G. T.)

But the Hampshire yeomen would not agree to this barbarity, and petitioned the king, who, reluctantly it is said, allowed the sentence to be changed to execution, which was carried out in the Square at Winchester in 1685.

Her body was taken home by her sorrowing countrymen, and she was buried in the church at Ellingham, across the main road from Fordingbridge to Ringwood, and near to the river. And there she lies in a tomb beside the south door, the flat stone recording that she 'Dyed the second of September 1685', her daughter, Anne Harfell, beside her.

St. Mary and All Saints is a pretty church of russet stone with a blue and gold painted sundial of 1720 above its porch, and an aged door — much pitted and cracked, but still sturdy after three and a half centuries of use.

From Broomy Walk comes the Linford Brook, past Poulner and into the Avon, fat and placid, flowing clear to the west of Ringwood, though the mill stream runs just into the edge of the market town, behind a new Industrial estate, the Riverside Country Club and old cottages.

Green farm-fields lie to the east, but the acid soil on the western edge makes it an area of heath and pine, with rhododendrons massing along the sides of the old undulating road that is first one side of the new A338 to Bournemouth and then the other.

Matchams Park has been given over to sport and leisure, with tracks for stock-cars and motor-cycling, a golf-course and the spread of a Sunday market; the cream-stone Matchams House is now a Country Sports Club, above a steep winding drive between dense banks of rhododendrons, glorious in daytime June, eerie in the winter dark.

Beyond, where the land flattens, gleam the runway lights of the Bournemouth International Airport, busy with regular and holiday flights within the United Kingdom, to the Channel Islands and Europe, and the custom of executive travellers unwilling to trust their business dealings to the vagaries of public transport.

Sir Alan Cobham first used the level fields at Hurn in the 1930s for his famous Air Circus, having been commissioned by Bournemouth Corporation to select a site for their proposed municipal airport; later, 1,000 acres were turned into a military aerodrome and opened in 1941 as part of 10 Group, Fighter Command, one of the south's important bases for fighter planes, bombers and transports.

With the return of civil flying at the war's end, BOAC made their home at Hurn, which served as the country's only international airport. The first time an intercontinental flight landed at the less important Heathrow, was because poor weather conditions at Hurn caused a Pan American aircraft to be diverted there.

The 1960s were some of Hurn's busiest years, and industry grew around the periphery of the airfield, including the building and maintenance of aircraft and training of crew and air traffic control; it was taken over by the Local Authority in 1969. The hangars of British Aerospace were at Hurn for many years.

During 1900, the airport handled nearly 9,000 tons of cargo, and more than 200,000 passengers.

Hurn is also the stage for an annual Air Show, and the Hawks of the exciting Red Arrows sometimes line up there ready for displays to delight their audiences, their vapour trails of red, white and blue drifting over the village of Sopley, down river.

The old Woolpack Inn sits beside a feeder brook of the Avon at Sopley, and into its yard until recent summers, clattered horses and riders of the Household Cavalry, a scene out of a Thomas Hardy novel except that the soldiers were in workaday khaki.

For horses need a holiday as well as soldiers, especially when their disciplined working life is spent on the hard streets of London, and for a few blessed weeks, the mounts and riders of the Lifeguards and the Blues and Royals left their ceremonial kit behind them and relaxed in the quiet of a disused R.A.F. camp at Sopley. But the land was sold and now their holidays are taken at Purbright.

If it were not for the little spire, which has been likened aptly to a candle-snuffer, passers-by might well miss Sopley's church, hidden as it is behind tall roadside trees; and that would be their loss, for it is well worth visiting.

With mellow russet walls, as at Ellingham, St. Michael and All Angels stands on a mound looking across to the long dark ridge of St. Catherine's Hill, itself standing between the Dorset Stour and the Hampshire Avon.

The Avon here is wide and deep and languorous, the fishing strictly private.

Parts of the Fisherman's Haunt Hotel at Winkton date from 1673, though there is nothing antiquated about today's facilities. Set back from the river by the quiet road from Ringwood to Christchurch, the public bars have a comfortable club atmosphere, with lovely views from tastefully decorated bedrooms.

When an extension was planned, workmen found a natural spring and a well which caused much interest. Since the well was exactly in line with the foundation trench, a bay-window was built round it, and the well was incorporated into the bar-room. Now it is a wishing-well feature for the benefit of local charities, and an electric pump raises spring water in a continual stream for an ice-cold addition to soft drinks and spirits.

Robert Southey, before he settled in the north-west and became one of the 'Lake poets', was very partial to the Avon. In his restless mid-twenties, newly married, but not enjoying the best of health, he sought seclusion from the hurly-burly of his London life and took a retreat at Burton, then in Hampshire.

It was 1797, and he revelled in the green peace, tramping up St. Catherine's Hill, making excursions into the 'simply lovely' New Forest, entertaining his friends, Charles Lamb among them, and writing poetry. His 'English Eclogues' were penned there, pastoral verses eulogising the countryside, including 'For the Banks of the Hampshire Avon':

> ' . . . *yon heathy hill*
> *That rises from a vale so green,*
> *The vale far stretching as the view can reach*
> *Under its long dark ridge, the river here*
> *that, like a serpent, through the grassy mead*
> *Winds on . . .*'

The hill is still heathy, the vale green, and wind on the river still does, though Burton has changed much and been built into a suburb; and Staple Cross, where once villagers gathered to listen to the canon's preaching, never recovered from the damage inflicted by an American jeep in wartime and is but a poor stump on its stone plinth, beside traffic rushing along the dual-carriageway to Christchurch. When Southey was there, his youthful high spirits led him to climb on the top step of the Cross, from whence he delivered a spontaneous discourse on the delights of the river valley that pleased him so well.

The home wherein he found happiness consisted of three cottages which he made into one, and there it is still, long and thatched, with low, dark rooms and the charm of many memories, beside an old, green garden.

Across the water-meadows from the dual-carriageway rises the bulk of Christchurch Priory, not quite in the spot first planned. For there is a tradition of a miracle at Christchurch, whose first name, long, long ago, was Twynham, town between two rivers.

Each day, the 12th century workmen carried their building tools to St. Catherine's Hill where the site was made ready, but by the start of each morning, they had been removed to the bottom of the hill.

And so it was decided to build at the second choice of site, and there they worked unhindered. A new workman joined the team, a stranger who ate no meals with the men, and claimed no pay. At the end of a weary day's work, a heavy beam was found to be a foot too short for its position in the roof, and the problem was shelved, as problems are, till the freshness of the morning. But when the builders gathered the next day, the beam was found hoisted into position; and the mystery man was seen no more. The miracle was discussed again and again, and the men decided that the Carpenter of Nazareth had been among them; and the name of Twynham was changed to Christ Church.

A charming tale, and a lovely old Priory, combining beauty and homeliness in the happiest way; and indeed it is a most attractive town, with nooks and corners and unexpected views.

The Normans built a castle there, the ruins remaining with five-foot thick walls, beside a tall chimney of the 'Constable's House', also a ruin but with good detail of domestic features of the day. Two branches of the Avon flow through the town, the mill stream making a third, as it edges Convent Walk at the foot of the Castle mound and round the Priory to the tiny Place Mill, a Domesday building, all making a delightful stroll.

The Constable's House and Christchurch Priory beside the Mill Stream. (G. T.)

And so the Avon waters mingle with the Stour at Christchurch Quay on the last stage of their journey to the open sea, and the river changes character in the brackish water below the Town Bridge.

The 150-acre wetlands of Stanpit Marshes edge the east of the harbour, a nature reserve since 1967, with tall sedge, and scurvy grass, rich in vitamin C and a boon to yesterday's sailors, sea lavender, and pink clumps of thrift, bright kingcups, round-leaved pennywort, irises and violets, blue forget-me-nots and the lovely warm russet of marsh-samphire in late summer.

The saltings and reed-beds are at the end of the migration flight-path marked by the course of the Avon, and ospreys can sometimes be spotted winging their slow majestic way above, with avocets occasionally joining the more plebeian inhabitants of the estuary, using the salt-marsh as a stop-over and sweeping their curved beaks swiftly through the muddy shallows.

Christchurch Harbour (G. T.).

Christchurch Harbour ends at the quay of Mudeford, where fishing-boats roll gently at their moorings and nudge against the grey sea-wall, their catches already away to the markets of the south — plaice, flounders, wrasse and mullet, brill and skate, turbot, bass and crab, and the famous Christchurch salmon from 'The Run', just inside the harbour mouth, some kept back for sale at the fresh-fish cabin on the quay.

Nets drape the railings, backed by lobster pots and coiled ropes, heavy anchor-chains and bright marker-buoys like toy balloons, and everywhere, the tang of salt and fresh fish.

A tiny motor-ferry plies from the quay on the east to the sandy dunes on the west, the headland rising beyond.

The Avon's adventures have come to an end; but for the explorers, pioneers and pirates, the soldiers and refugees, traders, merchants and artisans of perhaps five thousand years, who sailed and rowed and paddled their little craft past the great landmark of Hengistbury Head and up the shining river to the unknown — for those, adventure was just beginning.